BORN INTO WAR

BORN
INTO
WAR

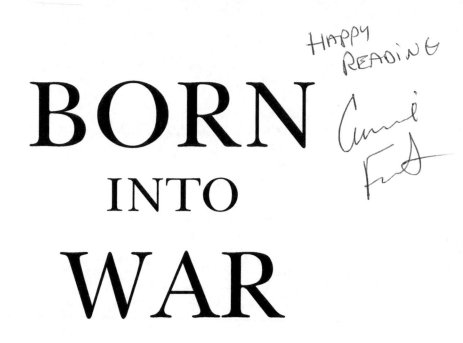

Happy Reading

CONNIE FORTIN
AS TOLD BY TRONG NGUYEN

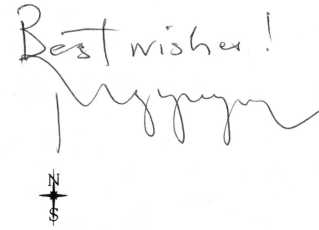

Best wishes!

NORTH STAR PRESS OF ST. CLOUD, INC.
St. Cloud, Minnesota

Connie and Trong wish to acknowledge the people who have given of time and advice in creating this book.
Editor: Carolyn Dindorf
Editorial Advice: Judy Hynes
Editing assistants: Christin Kjelland, Kseniya Voznyuk, Katie Farber
Trong's Song: Tom Broadbent
Story Contributors:
  Bichnguyet (Becky) Hoang
  Tan Nguyen
  Trang Nguyen
  Linda Rowan
  Roman Rowan
  Jeanne Teigen
  Joe Theis
Supporters: Two key people who contributed to the development of the book wish to be unnamed but are not forgotten.

ISBN-10: 0-87839-376-5
ISBN-13: 978-0-87839-376-3

First Edition, September 1, 2010

Printed in the United States of America

Published by
North Star Press of St. Cloud, Inc.
P.O. Box 451
St. Cloud, Minnesota 56302

www.northstarpress.com

info@northstarpress.com

Dedication

Ca and Kinh, Ron and Marilyn and all great parents.

Uncle Joe, Grandpa Tran and all of the soldiers.

The families separated by war and to the community leaders like Jeanne who helped bring them back together.

Acknowledgments

By Trong Van Nguyen
September 1, 2010

I would like to thank Connie, Carolyn, Chris, Roman, Ron, Marilyn, Katie, Kseniya and foremost Fortin Consulting Inc. for giving me the opportunity to express myself and helping me to complete this book. This experience has helped me greatly to get back in touch with my identity, roots and most important my culture.

I would also like to thank my family and friends for their love and support. If it wasn't for them I would not be who I am today. I'm fortunate enough to be brought up in a family with loving parents and siblings. My parents have always taught me to respect and help others when in need. Those are the life lessons and principles I live by every day.

My friends Pete, Donna, Jeff and Cameron, encouraged me to tell my story and helped me through the process. I appreciate their friendship and encouragement.

I would like to thank the higher power above for giving me the strength to go on. After fighting many struggles to come to America, I feel that I've won the life battle and have moved on with another chapter of my life. I now live in a freedom country that is filled with hopes and dreams. America is the place my parents and siblings wanted me to be.

And lastly, thank you Becky for being my best friend, standing beside me through the book writing and believing in me.

TABLE OF CONTENTS

Part III – America

Foreword

I was working one night at our restaurant, the Rose Garden. It was a slow summer night. An American woman came in for dinner. Instead of take-out she sat down and ordered. We started talking a little and for some reason I told her a bit about my life in Vietnam. I can't explain what happened next but the words just came out of my mouth and I asked her if she would write my book. She didn't seem to be paying very close attention to me but she nodded and said yes in between bites of her dinner.

I didn't know if she would remember me and the book promise. I didn't know her name or her phone number. I didn't see her for two months until she came to the restaurant with one of her colleagues. I asked her if she was ready to write the book. She had a funny look on her face and said "in November when my work is slower we will write the book". Her colleague, Carolyn, looked at her in disbelief. I found out later she owned a small company in Hamel and worked as many hours as I did.

In November she called and we arranged our first meeting at the Rose Garden after the busy dinner hour was over. She had given me an assignment over the phone to create a list of important events in my life so she could have an outline to start from. I was so excited, I worked on my list and I waited for our first meeting. My first list was in Vietnamese which didn't do her much good. She could only read English.

That night she came to the restaurant with her husband. My life partner was there as well. We learned each other's names, Connie, Roman, Trong and Bichnguyet (Becky). Before we began they ordered dinner. I couldn't stand the suspense. It seemed to take forever for them to eat their dinner. I had waited for this day for so long I just couldn't bear to wait a minute longer. I pulled a chair up to their table and started talking about my outline. Connie's laptop computer was on the other table. It wasn't time to start yet, but my story started to spill out. After about 10 minutes of speaking about the major events of my life, I felt like I might pass out. My mind was caught somewhere in the tragedy of the past. I went into a temporary shock. I just froze at their table unable to talk or move. Becky took me, put tiger balm under my nose and moved me away to some chairs by the cash register. The moment I had waited for, for so long was here but I couldn't be a part of it. Becky sat by Connie at her laptop and translated my outline and notes for her.

Connie and Roman were both very concerned and asked if I should go to the doctor. Becky knew better. She was familiar with what happened. She said "we have home remedies for this. Trong will be okay." From that night we met weekly for three months, Connie would ask me questions and I would tell her my story. We met either at the Rose Garden or at Connie's office nearby.

During our sessions we came to realize that both of us were born in 1960, the lucky year of the rat. We were exactly the same age. We were born on opposite sides of the world, yet we both owned small businesses in Hamel. Our life experiences in these past 47 years were drastically different yet something inside of us seemed to be the same.

At our last note taking meeting before Connie was going to start writing she looked at me strangely and said "Trong, why did you ask me to write this book? I can only guess you have asked everyone who came into the Rose Garden." I looked at her and said, "Many people have asked me the same question. I don't know why I asked you, but you are the only person I have ever asked to write my story." I told Connie, everyone asks me how much I have to pay you to write my book. I tell them you are not charging me to write my book. People say, 'Trong you are very lucky,' and I agree with them. But tell me,

Connie, why would you write this book for free, you didn't even know me?" Connie said, "I don't know Trong, I just am."

A moment of disbelief and wonder passed between us that night as we realized the enormous coincidence that resulted in this book being written. Connie set out to a remote cabin in Northern Wisconsin to start writing. When she came back she had a good start. Over the next year we met to clarify points and discuss particular issues. She gave me many drafts to review. The first time I read her writing, I cried when she described how I lost my mom and my dad. I have given some of the rough drafts to my family, friends and customers to read. Connie says, "Trong don't do this, it is still very rough." I don't care I love it.

Now my book is done. My story is told. I feel much better that my children and my grandchildren will know my story. The process of getting all of those secrets out has helped me heal. It is a big accomplishment for me, I am proud that I had the courage to stand up and tell my story.

Me signing the contract to have my book published and, more importantly, my story told.

PART I

LIFE IN VIETNAM

1

THE TAKE OFF

Ahhhhhh . . . *the seat is so soft and comfortable, cushioned on the back and the bottom. It reclines just a little.* People all around on every side of me talked in muffled voices, in many languages. I recognized some of them, Chinese, my native Vietnamese, and English. The people in front of me were getting their children comfortable. A woman in a blue uniform walked up and down the aisle helping people find their seat or a space for their bags. She stopped and talked to me too. I didn't understand what she said, so I showed her my ticket. She nodded and smiled and showed me how to fasten the belt on my chair. This was how I would be crossing the ocean, on this airplane with cushioned seats, with food and water, with bathrooms and air conditioning. I breathed deep, feeling my muscles relax and my eyes close. It was 1980 and my world was about to change . . . again.

A voice came across the airplane with an announcement in English, "Welcome aboard flight 2 to the city of Seattle, Washington, with connecting flights to Minneapolis-St. Paul. Please stow your luggage in the overhead compartment. If you have an item that doesn't fit in the cabin, bring it to the boarding door, and we will check it for you. Please take your seat and fasten your seatbelt." They were speaking in English, so I didn't understand what was being said. I looked around and watched the people next to me. They were checking their seat belts and putting away their books. I sat still, hoping I was doing the right thing.

The airplane crew was walking up and down the aisles, demonstrating how to put plastic masks over the mouth and nose while the voice continued, ". . . if there is a loss of cabin pressure, the panel will open, and oxygen masks will appear. Remain seated . . ."

I wondered what this was all about. I looked around, but none of the passengers were putting these masks on. I would just sit here and watch the others. After a while the voice stopped talking, and the lights were turned off. The plane was quiet except for the roar of the engines starting up.

The airplane started to back up, turn and soon was in a line of aircraft waiting to take off. I was in awe of all of these people riding in this airplane, in awe that I was riding in an airplane. Was it the first flight for the people next to me too? No one seemed too concerned. I had seen planes in the sky, small planes, and it made me shutter. I could still smell that, that odor of war . . . *Relax, relax,* I told myself that it was over. *Relax, relax . . .* I hummed a tune that my mother hummed when she was tired and still working. I had found myself humming this at times when I thought I could no longer go on. I was surprised that I was humming it now, now that I was in the comfort of this remarkable airplane. Perhaps it was because I had just said goodbye to the people I'd known this past year, and when the plane landed I would know no one.

The plane shook and threw me back in my seat. My ears felt a strange pressure that temporarily took my breath away . . . and we were airborne. Turning my head to peer out of the left-side windows, I saw only sky. To the right, through the rows of passengers I saw glimpses of the Hong Kong I had known this past 364 days. The buildings took on a new appearance as we turned and climbed into the sky. A tear rolled down my cheek as I offered a silent prayer of thanks to Ong Troi, my God up there.

One tear, another tear, and slowly I found myself transported back to the rainy season, the monsoons of South Vietnam. Back there we had two seasons, both of which were tropical and warm, the sunny season when people worked hard, and the rainy season where life was more relaxed. Those days it would rain so hard that I couldn't see a thing, but the storm would be over quickly. The air would smell fresh and clean, but the rain would be back soon. The rain would start again and stop again, on and off for days and weeks and months in a row.

2

MY FAMILY

I am a rat. Or rather I was born, according to the Chinese perpetual cal-
endar, in the year of the rat. The rat has been a lucky sign for me, although many people who have known me or my family might disagree
with this statement. Don't listen to them. As you read my story you can
judge whether the rat is a lucky sign or not. I was born in the small coastal
village of Tam Ich, Vietnam. Tam Ich is in the central part of South Vietnam
on the eastern seaboard. The entire country of Vietnam (North and South
Vietnam combined) is roughly shaped like an "S." Prior to 1975, South
Vietnam was a free country, and North Vietnam was a communist country.
Today the two countries have combined into one communist country. The
north and the south boundaries are gone, and the country is simply called
"Vietnam." My passport says that I am Vietnamese, but my heart says I am
South Vietnamese.

I was born during the Vietnam War on July 26, 1960. My mother,
Kinh Thi Ly (pronounced "King"), with the help of a local village
woman, gave birth to me in our small bamboo-and-mud house. I,
Trong Van Nguyen ("Tron"), was the fifth child and the second son
of my father, Ca Nguyen ("Ka"). My mother was thirty years old and
my father was thirty-two when I was born.

At the time of my birth, South Vietnam was democratic, and
North Vietnam was communist. The South Army was supported by
American troops. The North Army (referred to as the NVA) was supported by the Viet Cong. The Viet Cong were Vietnam citizens,
farmers, and ordinary people fighting for communism. They were
not uniformed, unidentified, and they were integrated into most of

3

the cities and villages. They were referred to as Pajama People; they were terrorists that worked at night attacking those siding with the South Vietnam Army.

Living in South Vietnam during this time was living a split life. During the day it seemed normal and safe, but during the night everything turned upside down, and nothing was safe. It was a scary place to be, but growing up, I didn't know any differently. Many mornings we would wake up to the carnage of war. I have many vivid images of this in my head, including the family of four living in our small village. Everyone thought they were communist supporters. One day they were gone. Rumor had it, they were off to work with the Viet Cong. Occasionally one of them would appear briefly in the village, perhaps to get supplies. About a year after they had disappeared, we woke to find all four of their dead bodies—the mom, dad, and two sons. Rumor had it that the North Vietnamese Army had been alerted that they were trying to return to the village, and they were ambushed during the night to stop their return and to keep the village safe. Everyone in my village observed, heard and experienced firsthand the horrors of this conflict. No one was protected from it.

In my family all of us children were given my father's name, Nguyen. This is pronounced "Win." I am glad my last name is Nguyen because I have always worked hard to win freedom, happiness, and safety for myself and my family. I believe being named Nguyen was a good omen for me. In my family the girls all had the middle name Thi, and the boys the middle name of Van. This is not so much a middle name as is common in other countries but an indication of your gender. My brother and sisters are: Oanh ("One") Thi Nguyen, born in 1946; Liet ("Lit") Thi Nguyen, born in 1952; Long Van Nguyen ("Long"), born in 1955; Nguyet Thi Nguyen ("Wit"), born in 1957; myself, Trong Van Nguyen, born 1960; and Hoa ("Wa") Thi Nguyen, born in 1962. If you were reading carefully you will know who my brother is. My oldest sister was born when my mother was sixteen years old. She was already fourteen, a young woman, when I was born. It was good that there were older children in the family because my mother needed much help. Oanh was like a second mother to me.

Our family lived comfortably in a house about 600 square feet in size. That is roughly the same size as a two-car garage. Remembering back, I can almost feel the bamboo shoots, hay, and mud that formed the walls of our home. The bamboo was smooth and jointed, light in weight and in color. If I really concentrate, I can remember the sweet grassy, earthen smell of my home. Back there your home was your home once you built it. There were no taxes or buying or selling of homes, probably because there was such little money. In our village of about 700 people our house was typical. The floor of our main house was cement although many people had dirt floors. It all depended upon how much money you had. We grew vegetables in a small garden next to the house: cilantro, tomato, mint, hot peppers, lettuce, bok choy, onions, and flowers too. I can almost taste those juicy red tomatoes as I think about them ripening in the sun. We had yellow fragrant flowers similar to marigolds. We saved the petals, and when they were dry we added them to hot water to make tea. Everything grew effortlessly in this sunny climate. Grass grew wild around our house; we didn't plant it. To keep it short, we cut it occasionally with a sickle, a curved blade on a stick. The sickle was used to harvest many plants and was a tool most households owned.

We had no running water, but we did have the river, a large river, nearly a city block wide as it ran into the ocean. The river ran fast during the rainy season. It was awesome, dangerous too. What I mean is we had no plumbing in our house. In fact the entire village of Tam Ich had no running water. This makes sense since the village had no well, no way of getting the salt-free groundwater to the surface.

The nearest source of fresh water was a well in a neighboring village, Phong Thanh, inland about a twenty-minute walk away. My older sisters would walk every other day to the well and carry water back for us. They carried it on a wooden pole with a wooden bucket on either end. This way the weight of the water was mostly on their shoulders and somewhat balanced. Five gallons of water weighs forty pounds. Five gallons of water does not go far for a family of seven people. On each trip they carried over fifty pounds of water. Carrying water was an industry in my village. If you could afford it, you would hire young people to carry water to you. Mostly the girls carried the water, and often they would make five or more trips a day to sell water to those who couldn't carry it themselves. We didn't waste fresh water.

Before we drank any water, my mother would boil it. This killed anything that might make us sick. Once it was cooked, we stored it in a covered container to protect it from contamination. I recall a time early on that my sister and I started playing in our drinking water barrel. We were splashing and laughing and cooling off. We got into serious trouble not only with my mom, but also my oldest sister who at a young age had to carry such heavy loads. We used fresh water very carefully, primarily for drinking and cooking, not for flushing the toilet. This is a joke of course. We had no toilets. Our bathroom was the ocean. Everyone in the village would go to a certain area away from the houses and fishing boats. If you were too young or too sick to walk to the ocean someone from your family would carry the waste to the ocean for you. The vast beautiful aqua blue ocean, the soft sandy beach, this was our septic system, our food source, our recreation, the center of our universe, and, ultimately, our escape.

3

The Food

Would you care for some refreshments—Coke, Sprite, juice, or coffee . . . peanuts?"

I had drifted off, trying to settle my nerves, thinking about my village, about my childhood. I hadn't lived in my village for nine years now. What was this woman asking me? "Orange juice?" Yes! I see other people with a drink and a snack, and I smiled and nod. She handed me a plastic cup with ice and juice and a small bag of nuts. Was I hungry? I guessed so. It has been many hours since my cousins, Thanh (pronounced "Tawn"), Hanh ("Hawn"), and I last ate at the Kai Tak Refugee Camp in Kowloon, Hong Kong. I looked into the plastic cup. Three small ice cubes floated in the orange liquid. Ice was an unusual, wonderful thing to me. It was cold and refreshing. We had it in my village once in a while, but it was a very big luxury. Ahhh, the juice tasted sweet and delicious, and the peanuts tasted salty and crunchy. I was in an airplane flying over the top of the world enjoying ice, orange juice, and peanuts.

The snacks we had in our village were quite different. Fruit was the most common snack. We often ate it before going to bed. My country was blessed with wonderful warm weather and rain that created variety and an abundance of fruit: coconuts, papayas, mangos, watermelons, jack fruits, and more. Jack fruit, big like a watermelon, had prickles all on the outside of it. When we cut it open, it was yellow, sweet and delicious. Sometimes we grew these in our yards, but more often they grew on farms.

Our meals were simple. My breakfast was often bread with sugar or sweetened condensed milk, although rice soup was common. The main staple of our diet was white, bleached rice. Rice was the difference between living and dying. It was more important than you can imagine if you live in a country of wealth. A bag of rice in your home, and you had no worries.

For our evening meal, we often had a bowl of rice for each person and a fried whole fish to share. We had a wide variety of fish since we lived right on the ocean and on the river. The fish came in all shapes and sizes: tipia, tuna, shrimp and many, many more. Fish was served looking like it did when it came from the ocean. Only the insides were removed. The head, eyes, fins and tail were all served and eaten at dinner. The eyes were a special treat, the best part of the fish. Fish sauce was the ketchup of Vietnam. This condiment was in everyone's household. It was made by fermenting fish. When the fish was fermented, the juice was strained from it, and a few simple ingredients were added to complete the sauce. The women took pride in who made the best fish sauce. Fish sauce never needed to be refrigerated since it was made from spoiled fish. Strangely enough, it tasted delicious.

Fishing was a big industry in Tam Ich. Not so much large industrial fishing, but simply small boats with nets or people with a fishing pole and a worm. You didn't need a fishing license to go fishing. The amount and type of fish you caught or the method you used were unregulated. If you caught more than one fish, you could try to sell or trade the extra fish to your friends or neighbors. Life jackets were not used. For all of the ocean fishing, there was not much protection for the fishermen except learning to swim. Many people lived on their boats. These boats were very small, much smaller than our home. Sunscreen in a bottle did not exist. We protected ourselves from the sun by wearing lightweight layers of clothes or leaf hats called Non La. The leaf hat is a well-known trademark of our country. It is a round cone-shaped hat made of leaves. It is the color of straw, and it protected us from the sun. The girls, women, and old men in our village wore this type of hat. Young men didn't. It wasn't cool. If the young men wore a hat, it was a baseball-type cap imported from China. Undoubtedly, if you see a painting of the Vietnam country side you will see people wearing leaf hats.

The weather was so temperate that we had no need for insulation in the walls of our homes or a furnace. We had no electricity, no glass windows, or weather stripping—not much of anything to keep the hot or cold air in or out of the house. The walls were for privacy and to keep the wind, rain, and cats and dogs out. The roof was the most important to provide shade and to keep us dry in the rainy season. We had no locks on the doors. In the morning, everyone opened the doors and the bamboo shutters that closed our open-air windows. Whoever woke up first opened up the door and windows. The windows were opened by propping up a stick to hold the shutter open. The shutter hinged from the top closing over the window in the night. The houses stayed open all day until the family went to bed. Even if no one was home during the day, the house would remain open. Snakes were common, but not as common as the insects found everywhere. Our village was a peaceful village, the people didn't have much money or many possessions, but it didn't seem to matter. Everyone sort of watched out for each other.

4

MY PARENTS

My head tipped sideways, and my body jerked, waking me up. The peanut wrappers had been cleared away, and a movie was showing. I couldn't hear the movie. It had no sound but it was a movie about a boxer training for a big fight. The woman next to me had earphones on similar to the ones in the pouch in front of my seat. I fiddled around with them enough to get some sound, and I changed the channels many times. I found English, Japanese and Spanish but not Vietnamese. I listened to some English, which I thought corresponded with the movie. I listened carefully to the words and tried to understand them. It was difficult. I took off the headphones and watched the movie in silence. I hoped I would be able to understand English well enough to get by. Thanh knew more English than I did. Maybe he could help. I hoped someone would be there when the airplane landed . . . I hoped I wouldn't get sent back to the refugee camp. I started humming my mother's tune.

All our beds were made out of wood and bamboo. The mattress was a thin mat made out of grasses. All the beds were enclosed with a tent-like drape of insect netting. Mosquitoes and other insects were very common in South Vietnam. There were zillions of bugs—so many that it was possible to never see the same type twice in a day. We didn't have tight-fitting windows, window screens, or doors to keep the bugs out, so instead we protected our beds. Our beds were the safest place in the house, so we often sat and played on our beds at night when the insects started to come in.

All the beds were shared. Sometimes I would sleep with my parents or my brother. My sisters would sleep together. This naturally led to squabbles. In one family I knew, the two girls kept fighting at bed-time. One girl wanted the pillow between her and her sister as if they each had separate beds. The sister didn't want the pillow there. This went on for several nights. Finally their dad had had enough. Since there wasn't room for more beds, he took a knife and cut the blanket in two pieces. "There you go" he said. "You each have your own blankets. Pretend you have your own bed. No more fighting."

As a youngster I preferred to sleep in the hammock chair we had strung inside our home between the window frames. I dreamt of being in the Navy and sleeping on a ship. I looked out the window and saw the stars in the night sky and imagined my life as a man. My parents asked me why I liked to sleep like this, and I would tell them. They would smile and let me be. I wonder if they prayed for my safety.

My father, Ca, was the oldest son in his family, a position of importance in our culture. He worked for the South Vietnamese government as a high school teacher, He taught a variety of classes, such as French, math, and history. In my country, there were two types of schools, public and private. Until ninth grade, they were all public schools. Starting at ninth grade, there were also private schools. Anyone could attend a private school as long as you could pay. When you no longer could pay, you would drop out of school and that would be the end of it. No one forced you to go to school. There were no laws requiring it. The public school was free, but you had to take a test and get good enough marks to be selected to attend this school. My father taught at the private school, but my sisters and I attended the public schools. All of us were good students . . . well, my sisters were better students. They took their studies more seriously than I did. School was a big part of everyone's world. No matter if you attended a public or private school, every student wore a uniform. It was amazing for such a poor country to have this convention.

My dad's school, Dang Khoa, was located in a nearby city called Nha Trang (pronounced Na Tran). During the week, he stayed with my Aunt Tha and Uncle Dung. On the weekends, he came home to the village. When he was teaching, we didn't see him very much. When I was two, my youngest sister, Hoa Thi Nguyen, was born. We now had a family of eight. This was a crowded but brief moment in our family history, for, shortly thereafter, my sister Oanh got married and moved to the city, leaving my mother with the primary duty of raising and protecting five children in the middle of the Vietnam War.

While my dad was away, my mom worked hard. Mom was a quiet person. She was a serious business woman. She had a small store attached to the front of our house. This wasn't a store you could walk in, but more of an addition to our home. It was built out of mud and bamboo. It had a counter that people would walk up to and look to see what she had for sale. My dad did not get involved in her business, nor did he bring supplies for her to the village on his return trips from teaching school. She was in charge.

There was always something for sale, but it varied depending on what she could find. It could be something she grew or cooked or made, like bananas, coffee, coconuts, soup, Coca Cola, soap, candy, beer, a glass of wine (not a bottle), rice, tiger balm (an aromatic medicinal ointment), cigarettes, (not a pack, just one or two), or cookies. The selection rotated. It all was strictly off limits to us.

My mother was always busy and, because of her business, she wasn't home a lot. She traveled to buy things to sell at her store. She commuted on a three-wheeled small bus packed with people and all of their belongings. She would have to walk a distance on the narrow, country roads to catch a ride and travel on this bus to the city.

My sisters would help her on her buying days or run the store while she was away. From this they quickly learned how to deal with money or *dong*, the Vietnamese currency. (In 2010, one U.S. dollar equaled 19,600 *dong*.) The older kids watched out for the younger kids. I never felt neglected, I always felt loved by my family. In all the years I lived with my mother, I never saw her play, or relax. She always worked. Work was her hobby and her life. I think she was content. She was always looking for a way to make ends meet.

My mother's dad, my grandfather, had passed away before I was born, so I never had the pleasure of meeting him. My grandmother lived in Ninh Hoa a city a few miles north of Tam Ich. She had the kindness and toughness in her that I could see in my mother, and that I can feel in me. She had much less money than my other grandparents and thus a harder life. I loved her deeply. My mother, their eldest daughter, was the apple of my grandmother's eye.

I remember the day Hoa was born, or maybe I just remember hearing stories about her birth. I was only two at the time, and I am sure I was a handful to the rest of the family. It was a day similar to the others, warm and sunny, and my mother was very pregnant. This pregnancy was more difficult for her since she was thirty-two, compared to her first delivery at sixteen. She seemed more tired and weary. Who could blame her, she deserved to be tired from keeping track of five kids, worrying about her husband and keeping her business running.

My older sister ran across the village to find the birthing woman. My mom lay down and instructed the children to go outside. The atmosphere felt different. My sister returned home with the village woman and went inside. Later that night, I saw Hoa for the first time, a tiny baby. I was no longer the youngest member of my family. I felt proud. I do not remember how my mother recovered from this, but I'm sure my sisters helped out tremendously. Nursing was the mainstay in the baby's diet, and keeping my mother nourished, rested and hydrated was important. I know I didn't help in the resting department.

As the war escalated near our village, my dad became more politically involved. He did not want to leave my mom and us home alone. He quit his teaching job just after Hoa was born because he didn't want to live away from the family. Prior to his resignation from his teaching post, the school had not been able to pay him on a regular basis. He needed to find other ways to help support all of us once he left his teaching position and was in the village full time. We were thrilled to have him home with us. He soon became the mayor of our village. We don't call it mayor, but it is similar in that the people voted for him. There was a good deal of trust and respect for my dad from our community, even though our village was small and inconsequential compared to most. Being a figurehead in the South government, my dad was a target for the North Vietnamese Army (NVA).

My country changed, subtly at first then at a more rapid pace. The South Vietnamese government seemed to be in control during the light of day and people went about their business. However, as night fell the communists came out of the hills and the jungle and terrorized South Vietnam. The nights were long and evil. Most every night, something happened, someone disappeared or was shot or robbed, raped or beaten. The Viet Cong usually came in small groups. No one could predict where they would show up next. We never understood they wanted to change our country or disturb our small villages? We were humble peaceful people. Wondering how long would this go on?

Being the mayor, my dad was at greater risk. To be safe, most men in my village stayed in the village during the day and went to the city of Nha Trang at night to hide and to help the South Army. In the black of night, the Viet Cong, who might have been our friends or neighbors, worked their evil. They put on dark clothes and fought for the communists. It was hard to know who was who. There were traitors to South Vietnam all mixed in with the rest of us. For the American troops working in South Vietnam, recognizing the Viet Cong was impossible. Sometimes we knew or sensed who the traitors were, the bad guys. The Americans did not. We all looked the same, and even though the Viet Cong might be friendly with them during the day, they would ambush them in the evening.

Ever since I was born, our family would fish towards evening. The air was cooler then, and the fish easier to catch. Despite the dangerous situation, the tradition continued. Often my dad would take my second sister, Liet, out fishing in the evening. They used a small boat made of woven bamboo coated with tar to seal out the leaks. If they heard any noise in the bushes, they would get really quiet because they knew the Viet Cong were near. Often they hid in the small boat, under the gnarled mangrove trees that grew on the water's edge. One night my dad and Liet didn't return. It was a sleepless night for my mom. The next morning, we learned that my dad chose to abandon the boat and run into the dark jungle to hide. Somehow from where they were hiding they could tell that the Viet Cong were looking for them under the mangrove trees. They stayed still until the bright sun of morning when they could safely return home. When they returned, Liet, still a child, asked my dad, "Why go through this? Why not go to Nha Trang each night to hide and be safe like the rest of the men?" My dad said he had nothing to hide, he was a good man and had done nothing wrong. He did not want to go to the city and hide. He wanted to be with his family.

Some of the scariest nights were those during the monsoon. Those nights were so black and dark and the rain came down so hard you could not see your own hand in front of your face. It was so loud you could not hear anything but the pounding rain and the pounding of your heart. There was no way to see or hear someone sneaking up on you.

My father was a brave man. He made all of us feel brave too. He was also a very smart man, an educated person. My dad's parents lived pretty close to us. They were a proper family, a wealthier-than-average family—some considered them rich. I never heard my dad swear or use bad language. He never was rough or mean to us or my mother. He was an outgoing person, a good man. People looked up to him and respected him. Many of my relatives and people from my village have told me that I have many of his qualities. I feel very proud of this. It is the greatest compliment I could receive.

5

Our Home

"Chicken or Beef, Chicken or Beef . . ." The movie was finished, the lights were on and dinner was being served. How strange to be eating above the clouds. I was nineteen years old, and this was going to be my first meal with silverware instead of chopsticks. How odd, yet how wonderful to have a hot meal brought and served to you in your seat. I folded down the little table hidden in the chair back directly in front of me. The woman in blue was still smiling at me and offered me a dinner. I was not sure if I had the chicken or the beef, but it was salty and delicious. I ate it awkwardly with my silverware. I stabbed my meat with the fork, and ate it as if it were on a stick. I hoped no one was watching too closely. I needn't have worried. Everyone seemed to be enjoying their own meal. If only this flight would never end. This was the most comfortable surroundings I had had as far back as I could recall. This must be how the rich and famous people lived, quite unlike the open space of the village, and the smells of the village, the smells of my mom cooking dinner.

In Tam Ich, our cooking area was separated from the rest of the living area. It had its own small house. The two houses were connected by a roof. It was under this roof that we ate our meals—in the open air yet protected from the rain. We had lanterns to provide light as needed, and we used them every night in the house. My family had no pets, but many people did. Dogs and cats were common in Vietnam. I had heard stories of people in other countries where the pets live in the house, even some that sleep on the bed. I have heard that some people bring pets to the doctor when they are sick. In my country pets lived outdoors. Everyone enjoyed seeing them, and most would pet them, but that is about it. The pets in my neighborhood would often be seen walking around sniffing here and there or, if it was raining, lying in people's open air dining rooms. Occasionally they would run in the house, and someone would chase them out. Pets had to find their own food if they needed more than the scraps their owners threw to them. The family must be fed first and often this was a big task. The pets were quite self-sufficient.

The kitchen or cooking area was separated from the rest of the living area for a few reasons, one being to keep the smoke out of the rest of the house. We had no automatic range, microwave, or oven. To cook, we burned wood, coal, corn, or whatever we had. We worked to find a steady, dependable source of heat. There were no emission standards or safety codes. Life was based on more immediate survival needs and making ends meet. There was no welfare system; the government did not take care of anyone. It was up to the family members to take care of each other. Even if you were distant cousins, you were obligated to help your relatives if you were able. Charity was very rare. There was no concept of giving money to the hospital to help unknown people. All money and resources were directed towards your own family.

In my village most people traveled by foot. They walked where they wanted to go. It was about a two-mile walk to the nearest road that had motorized traffic. If we wanted to go to another village or into the city, we would catch a ride on a bus. The bus traveled only on the larger roads. No buses came to our village. The buses we had were more like a truck with benches in the back. The driver and one other sat in the front compartment. The back compartment was for passengers. It was open air or covered by a canvas. People who could not fit in the back would stand on the bumper of the bus and hang on to a pole. This was very dangerous, and many people got hurt riding buses in this way.

There was no set of official stops. Communication between driver and passengers was informal. Often the bus didn't really stop but just slowed down for people to get on or off. Bicycles and motorcycles were also common in Vietnam. Some people in my village had pedal bikes. No one that I knew had a motorcycle. Everyone in the city, or so it seemed, had motorcycles. Sometimes the streets were so crowded with motorcycles that you could almost touch knee to knee.

One day when my mom was playing around with us she told us of an adventure she and my dad had. They decided to take a ride into the city. Since they had only one bike, my dad was giving my mom a ride on his bike. Indeed a long ride. Something happened along the way, and my mom got mad and jumped off of the bike. My dad, who was in front, kept talking to her like she was still riding. By the time he figured out she wasn't there and stopped the bike, she was nowhere in sight. My mom started walking back on this vast desolate road, and she became scared and started crying. When my dad turned the bike around and found her, she wasn't mad at him anymore but happy to see him again. I think it must be true love to pedal a bike for another person for such a long journey.

I finished up my fine airplane meal with a cup of tea. I was feeling much better and more relaxed. Maybe I had just been hungry. After the trays were picked up, I unbuckled my seatbelt and stood up. I wiggled my way in front of the people in my row and made my way to the bathroom at the rear of the plane. I scanned the rows of people, wondering where they were going and where they came from. I smelled tiger balm coming from somewhere in the back of the plane. It smelled good. Could the other passengers tell that today was a big day for me? I waited in line for the restroom, and I soaked in the surroundings, the smell of coffee, the sound of people talking in other languages, and the nothingness out the window of the plane.

It seemed funny that a person could walk around just as normal as could be while flying in a plane. It felt good to stretch my legs. I wasn't used to sitting still this long. The last time I sat still for a long period of time was without doubt, the worst days of my life. The hair on my arms raised just thinking about it. I started humming as I made my way back to my seat after using the luxurious restroom. I was happy to be seated and strapped in again. The softness of the seat hugged my skinny body. I put some tiger balm on the back of my neck to loosen up my stiff muscles. I pulled the small airplane blanket up over me and relaxed.

6

The Capture

I heard the sound of my mother wailing and crying. She was inconsolable. My older sister Liet was trying to calm her, to talk to her. My mother was pacing and thrashing around, her hands pulling on her hair over and over again. It was night time in South Vietnam, and it was 1963. The Vietnam War was in full swing. My baby sister was not quite one year old and I had just turned three. Our country had become one by day and another by night.

On September 12, 1963, my cousin Ra ("Raw") led the Viet Cong soldiers to our home. My dad stared with disbelief and hatred at my cousin as the Viet Cong took him from our house. As a child, it didn't make sense to me, but my mother's reaction was unprecedented. I could tell something was terribly wrong. I sensed my mother would never be the same. A piece of her had gone with my father, and a piece had stayed with us. She was split in half. In the days following my dad's capture, nothing was right. Chaos and panic rang through the village and our home. My mother was despondent, and we were filled with fear.

Ra was my first cousin on my mother's side. He was always a little different than the rest. He wanted to be important. He didn't listen, and he was selfish. There were these types of people in many families— nothing could be done about that. I had not heard any mention of Ra prior to my dad's kidnapping. It must have been something the adults would talk about amongst themselves. I learned later, after I came to investigate this situation, that when the South army found out my cousin was spying, he took off for the woods. The South people knew he had sided with the Viet Cong some time before my dad's disappearance. I doubt that anyone would have thought a family member would turn on another, especially on my father. After that horrible night we didn't see any more of my cousin for five years. In 1968 he came back but just for a short while.

Every day we looked for signs of my dad. Many people in the village and the city looked too. No one knew how to find him. We hoped he would escape and find his way back to us. We never heard of his death. We kept praying for his safe return. We would listen to every little noise, but my dad never came back.

That same year, shortly after my dad's capture, my mom delivered still-born twin boys. The sadness in our house continued. My brothers were buried in the local cemetery.

I often try to remember a little more about my dad, what he looked like, the sound of his voice, and the feeling of him picking me up and twirling me around the garden. I am filled with a sense of loss because I cannot remember much of him. My sisters tell me I am a lot like him. Maybe that will help me remember more. It is up to me to find out what happened to him. Some day, I promise myself, I will find out. Someday we will know what happened to my father.

How my mother survived those years is a miracle to all of us. She never was a complete person after my dad was abducted from our home. She had a sadness that my people described as a split or broken heart. Without help from my father, my oldest brother, Long, should have been in charge. Tra-

My father, Ca Nguyen.

dition dictated this. But he was still quite young, only eight at the time of my father's disappearance. The responsibility for all of us was on my mom and older sisters. My oldest sister was already married and living on her own in the city. She thought of us often and tried to do what she could to help, but it was difficult since she was far away. Her husband worked in an ice factory and they lived in the housing provided to the employees. It was a big tin building, much different than our bamboo house in the village.

My mom didn't tease or joke much anymore, but one day something in the kitchen broke. It must have struck her funny because she teased me that there was a man in the house, but he didn't fix anything. I was only a little guy and wasn't too useful yet. She was teasing me, and I could tell and enjoyed that, but I was still too young to fully understand the predicament she was in.

When I was four years old, we entered the first holiday season without my father. There had been some Christmas celebrations in the village, but very brief. Christmas was a Christian holiday, and we were Buddhist. Although the celebrations extended beyond the church, our family didn't really join in. The most exciting part of the celebrations were the people camping outside of the Catholic Church for the few days surrounding December 25th. It looked interesting, and I thought it would be fun to do, yet we never did. Anyone could camp, even non-Catholics, but it wasn't a very strong tradition. My observation was that the lights stayed on all night, and people walked and talked outside. Christmas tended to fall on a warm and beautiful night. It wasn't at all like Christmas celebrations in much of the world with pine trees, snow, Santa Claus, and gifts. It was a commonly skipped over, incidental holiday here.

February 13, 1964, was the first Chinese New Year celebration without my dad. Vietnam is very close to China, and the Chinese had a major influence on our culture. This is why the Chinese New Year was so important. Everyone celebrated it. Realizing my father would not be around this New Year made my mother more withdrawn. I could hear her humming almost wherever she went. It worried her as to how she would get money to put in the red envelopes for us children. She was sure my dad's parents, Ngu and Thiet, would have red envelopes for us and so would her mother, although she probably could not afford very much. This year she might have to sell some of her possessions to get a few *dong* for the envelopes. Everyone, no matter how poor, found a way to put a few *dong* in the small red envelopes for at least their own children. As the Chinese New Year approached, the village would begin to celebrate and continue celebrating for several days. There would be flower stands, food of all sorts, and music. The war would be temporarily forgotten and fun and laughter would spread across the village.

Grandpa Ngu and Grandma Thiet.

7

THE TEMPLE

As a small child I was sent many days to the Tam Ich Buddhist temple in our village. My mother insisted that I go. I did not attempt to negotiate with my mother. I did as I was instructed, not so much because I wanted to, but because it meant survival. My brothers and sisters and I were not waited on or coddled as in many other cultures. We grew up fast. I didn't look forward to going to the temple. I would have rather chased the cats and dogs out in the yard or stayed near my mom, but I had no choice.

I walked to the temple one or two times a week until 1966 when I was six years old and old enough to walk to school. Most days Hoa and Nguyet accompanied me. As a small child I was able to help out around the temple. My teacher showed me how to do some cleaning and some church related functions such as lighting the incense or helping with the collection box. People would come and meditate cross-legged on the floor or bow and kneel to pray. Some days were busier than others. On special days like New Years, the temple was crowded.

I learned by watching and being a part of background activities. I can still hear the *thump, thump, thump* of voices blended together in rhythmic praying each morning. It was so loud, people could hear it from outside. To some it was annoying, but to most of us, it was a familiar, comforting sound. Many people in Vietnam are Buddhist. During my time at the temple, I observed and participated in the praying and chanting rituals, I found it to be a soothing, predictable part of my day. Sometimes it got a little boring. My attention seemed to wander out the window or to whatever was making the most noise.

At the temple I learned some traditional healing skills like relaxing a cramp or stiff neck. I also found out what happens when you have a serious toothache. The tooth is pulled out. There was no dentist. None of us had ever heard of one, or visited one. The day I observed a tooth pulling, one of the older men was sitting on the floor and had his jaw in his hands. A few of the older people stopped to look in his mouth and talk to him. They gave him some Chinese medicine powder I hadn't seen before. About an hour later, they came back with a string and tied it around his tooth, real tight. One person held his jaw and the other pulled. The tooth came out with just a few strong pulls. They gave him something to put in his mouth to bite down on. By the end of the day he seemed much better. I know I spent much of that day staring at him hoping to see his tooth or the lack thereof.

Chinese traditional medicine was used both in the temple and at home to help people with a variety of health problems. Most of it was derived from plants grown in our area. We used Chinese medicine at my house too. Western medicine existed in Vietnam, in the larger cities, but not in my village. My mom didn't go to a hospital to deliver my sister. There wasn't a western medicine facility or doctor's office in our village. People who were experts with Chinese medicine made and sold some of their remedies. They also were available to help diagnose a problem and recommend a treatment. No one I knew had ever visited a western doctor or a dentist.

The majority of the common ailments and treatments where taken care of by the family. People did not take a Tylenol for a headache, but rather would rub tiger balm on their head. This also was used if you had a backache or stomachache or felt faint. The jelly would be rubbed on the affected area. If you had a cough, a mixture of fresh ginger and water was brewed for you to sip. If any of us had a fever, we would try to hide it from my mom. If she knew we were sick in this way, she would make us take a small spoon of this mixture she had in a yellow jar. It was so strong tasting and icky it made me shudder. Only a piece of sweet sugar candy would help take this taste from my tongue. Nothing I have tasted since then can quite compare to the fever medicine she gave us. If I had to imagine what would be in this syrup I could guess rotten tree roots and animal hind ends. That makes me smile. My mom would scold me for making up such a story, but she would smile too.

SCHOOL

We hit a tiny pocket of turbulence, and I opened my eyes. In my mind I could still clearly see my mother. I can see her sitting with us all at the outside table serving us rice and listening to our banter. I could hear her telling me to be a good boy as she smoothed my hair. I was happy for the memories so sharp and clear. I felt lucky to have had such good parents. I hoped someday that I would be a good parent too. I wondered about my girlfriend, Hong, if she knew what happened to me. I wondered if she had had our baby, if she was okay?

The people in front of me were moving around a bit. The kids were getting restless. It had been a long flight, and we were only halfway there. The little one stood in his seat and looked over the top at me. I smiled and wiggled my fingers at him. He grinned and hid. Soon he was back looking over the top of the seat again. We played this way back and forth, his blond hair going in many directions. My dark hair might be going in many directions too. It had been awhile since I combed it. I winked at him, relishing the distraction. I had always enjoyed little kids.

In the years since my fathers' disappearance, my mother told me many times, "Trong be a good boy, a good person. Go to school, never quit school, and keep on learning." She told me I must be a confident person. There were steps to this. The first step was the influence of the family. The parents must teach a child right and parents must be good. The children would turn out like their parents. The second step was school. I must seek out good teachers and good friends. When the teacher described the fish, the color, the size and so on I could think about it and learn from them. The third step was to be observant. I must go outside and see how things work. I could see the fish the teacher described and so much more. Learn with my own eyes how the fish swam and where it lived. Touch the fish, see how it felt. Be observant, I can learn much by watching and listening. I do not need to be told everything. It was not possible.

My mother, Kinh Thi Ly.

I can hear my mother saying, "Trong, keep the company of good people, and stay away from bad people." She said it all of the time. I guess she thought I wasn't listening. It was often true that the young people who lost their parents turned out bad. It was very common in Vietnam during the war. Youth, filled with anger, turned into thieves, or got involved in gangs and stole things or started using drugs like cocaine. I didn't want to turn bad. I wanted to be in school. I saw the ones on drugs with the needle tracks. I didn't like this. It scared me. I never wanted to be like this.

When I was six years old, I was finally old enough to go to school. I was elated. I had watched my brother and sisters go off to school for years. My youngest sister, Hoa, was heartbroken when she had to go to the temple, and I got to go to school. I felt bad for her. Since my dad was a school teacher, school was taken seriously in our home. I remember the day my mom presented me with my first school uniform, blue pants and a white shirt. They were hand-me-downs from a bigger boy, but I didn't care. I was so proud. It was 1966, and the Viet Cong and North Vietnamese were still working to take over South Vietnam. We had American troops helping protect our country, and we survived the best we could under such unusual and taxing conditions. At home we always spoke Vietnamese to each other, never any other language. At school we were introduced to English in a very minute way. We didn't take it too seriously, although there was more interest than usual since the American soldiers were in our country. We learned simple words like "hi" and "yes," and we could count to ten. We didn't think much about it.

On school days, my mother often sent us with a lunch. Some of my classmates lived close enough to walk home for lunch, but we lived too far away. Our typical lunch was rice and a bit of something else, maybe a fruit or vegetable or bread. The school had fresh water for us to drink, and we took full advantage of this, drinking plenty of water each day. Some days my mom would send me a small amount of money instead of a lunch. In front of our school was a good assortment of street vendors selling many delicious types of food and drinks. We didn't have much money but could buy some rice, meat, or a bun. It was always delicious and a treat when we were sent with money instead of a lunch. Some days I didn't make the smartest choices and would buy a sweet drink or candy instead of lunch. I didn't do that too often because I got so hungry by the end of the day. Also, Long would tell my mom if he found out, and that would make her unhappy.

Soccer was a popular sport played by many of us as we grew up. We didn't have organized leagues, very good fields, or equipment, but it was fun and good exercise. It helped keep us all out of trouble. We would play hard, imagining we were famous soccer players, and run with our arms above our heads when we scored a goal.

When I was seven years old, the American soldiers built us a water tower. It had a long pipe that went all of the way to the well in the next village. This brought fresh water into our village, and no one had to carry the water anymore. We still transported water from the water tower to our homes, but compared to the journey to the next village it was nothing. This was great news for me because I never had to carry the heavy water from the next village. I was too young and now, for the first time ever, we had a source of fresh water in our village.

Life continued on this way with us going to school, the temple, and my mom working. In 1968 my second sister, Liet, moved away from home. She was sixteen years old and finished with school. She went to live with my oldest sister, Oanh, and her husband, Tu Do. Liet got a job working for my aunt in Nha Trang which was about fifteen miles from us, a long journey. I missed her greatly. She spent a lot of time with me when our mother was busy working and I relied on her for many things. Now my dad, Oanh, and Liet were all gone at least on a daily basis. Our house was changing. My brother Long was getting older. He was thirteen years old now and taking on more responsibility for the family. I really looked up to him. He was like a hero to me. Now that I was eight years old, I had an increasing share of household tasks too.

Long never had a birthday party. No one in Tam Ich had a birthday party, but I had heard about them. I knew that they were common in many parts of the world and that rich people in Vietnam had birthday parties. Most of us didn't know our exact birth date. When parents went to register the birth of their child, which could be days, weeks, or months after the birth, the registrar often marked the papers and recorded the information with the current date, not asking the actual date of birth. It never really mattered to us. From what I had heard, a birthday party sounded fantastic, too good to be true. None of us had a birthday present or any sort of a celebration for our birthdays.

As our family was shrinking, in Nha Trang, Oanh's family was growing. Oanh was expecting her first child. Oanh was twenty-two years old when she gave birth to my nephew Thanh, the first grandchild for my mother. My mother was happy for Oanh and her husband. She was happy that Liet was there to help with the new baby, but she was sad that my dad might never see his grandson, and she was sad that she was so far away from them. Nevertheless, she told everyone in the village about her new grandson, and it seemed to fill her spirit with happiness.

The first day that Oanh brought the baby to visit us, our home was filled with joy. Each of us took turns holding him, walking him around and talking to him. We sat in the open air eating area enjoying the perfect weather. Neighbors and friends came in small groups to welcome Oanh back and congratulate her on her baby boy. Hoa was six years old already, so we hadn't had a baby in the house for a while. Hoa's eyes twinkled as my sister handed her the tiny baby to hold. It was a good day for our family, and it was a good year for Hoa because she was finally old enough to join me at school. My mom, for the first time in twenty-two years, had no children at home. All six of us were either in school or out on our own.

9

A BIRTHDAY PARTY

The people next to me on the airplane were having a lively discussion. They were speaking English and, although I had studied it on and off for years, I still was not good at it. I could read English better than I could listen and understand it. We tried to visit with each other a little earlier on the flight, and it seemed to go okay. The woman next to me reached into her bag and pulled out a small package wrapped with foil paper and a purple bow. She handed it to the woman next to her and started singing to her in a soft voice. The other woman seemed very surprised and pleased. I was proud of myself because I had figured out what was going on, a birthday party!

I was fascinated by the birthday party taking place in the seats next to me. The woman sitting two chairs over was opening her gift, a beautiful silk scarf with yellow flowers silk screened on it. It reminded me of the yellow flowers in our yard. I wondered if they knew how good these flowers smelled or that you can make tea out of them. I pointed to the flowers and tried to describe them to the women. They seem interested. The words were coming slowly, and my pronunciation was bad. The women next to me took out some paper and pen and, between pointing, speaking and writing, I was able to describe the flowers to them. I was a part of the birthday party. The woman next to me introduced herself as Georganne and told me Lisa was the woman two seats down. To my surprise, Georganne reached into her bag one more time and took out some colorful paper napkins and a small package of little cakes. The three of us ate cakes on the airplane way over the Aleutian Islands.

10

LAST DAYS OF TAM ICH

The same year my first nephew was born, my cousin Ra came back to South Vietnam. His return caused a stir of emotions and a ripple of concern throughout the village. We never saw him, he never talked to us, and he stayed out of our way. My mom had strict orders for us to stay away from him. His return caused a bout of depression, fear, and anger in my mother. The last time anyone had seen him had been the day he led the Viet Cong to our home and took my dad away. We never knew why he joined the Viet Cong or why he came back, but when he returned, he surrendered to the South Vietnamese government. He told the South Vietnamese Army to go back to the mountain to get the communists. When he joined the South Army, he led the troops to the communists. Together they went out after them. Fortunately for him, his assignment with the South Army was in an area away from our village. I was not sure that he would have survived very long in our village.

During my grade-school years, my days were occupied with walking the forty-five minutes or so to school each day, learning, and walking back. This was no problem except in the rainy season. By the time I got to school, I was soaking wet. As I grew older and realized my dad wouldn't be around to make me go to school, I started skipping school a few times here and there and then more and more. I would just wander around. I always made sure I would go to school on the days with the celebrations. On these days we would get a small sack with a pencil and maybe some candy. One time my teacher took me by the arm and said, "No, you skip school too much. You cannot have the treat bags. Only the good boys and girls who come to school can get these." My sisters were much better about attending school every day. Somehow I had trouble getting into the spirit of it.

The route to school was well worn with the footsteps of many children over the years. If someone got hurt or sick, there was generally an adult or an older child along the way that would take them under their care and make sure they got home again. When we wore shoes, they were sandals, but often we wore no shoes. The bottoms of our feet grew thick like leather and it was really quite comfortable to walk long distances without shoes. Nobody in the village wore stockings or had tennis shoes. The evenings would be spent playing soccer by the temple or helping my mom or sisters. On days where there was no school, we would go swimming in the ocean and lay on the soft sand to relax and warm up.

Da da dum, da daa da dum. I could hear that same tune over and over again. My mom was having difficult times running her business and the house without my two oldest sisters. She was sad many days and, although she didn't cry, her spirit seemed to be broken. As a boy much of this didn't register with me. I was on my own path of school and learning, war and friends. The struggle between the North and South continued and influenced everything in our world. We often talked about when we would join the army. As long as we stayed in school, we were not required to serve in the army, but if we quit school, we were immediately enlisted in the ARVN (Army of the Republic of Vietnam). My older brother was sixteen years old, and my mom was very worried that he would quit school and join the army. My sisters had been trying to get us all to move to the city with them. They said there was more opportunity there, it was safer for us, and we could all be back together again. I think they were very worried about my mom. My mom loved us deeply, and she still worked very hard, but she didn't seem quite the same as she did a few years earlier. We wondered if it was because she missed my dad, if she was worried about the war and daily violence, or if she was sick. She never talked to us about any of these things.

NHA TRANG

In 1971 my sisters finally convinced my mother to move the whole family to the city of Nha Trang. The day before we left, we wandered through town saying our goodbyes. We felt happy, confused, and sad yet on a slow mission forward. We didn't sell our home in the village when we moved; we just left it empty. No one had any money, so no one could have purchased it. Other people from our village just moved in and lived in our vacated house. Often a several-generation family crowded in their own house would split up and spread out. That was how it worked. We left with no picture of our house in Tam Ich, but it looked much like the other bamboo houses all over Vietnam.

As we moved to the city to be near my sister, we were leaving a part of us behind . . . including the time spent with my father. My mother packed us up with everything we could carry, and we left town. Long, Nguyet, Hoa, my mom, and I walked out of the village and along the road where we would eventually find a bus. We arrived in Nha Trang when I was eleven years old, hoping for a better future. As much as we tried to remain optimistic, a better future was difficult to imagine with the war escalating in our country.

My two oldest sisters were working for my Aunt Tha in a big rice warehouse and were much relieved that we were moving to Nha Trang. Liet was married now and expecting her first child. I was looking forward to getting to know my cousins Thanh and Hanh. They were a few years older than I, but my mom assured me we would become good friends.

My aunt and sisters were waiting for us when we got off the bus and showed us to our new living quarters. My aunt and uncle owned

My Aunt Tha and her husband.

a piece of land where they built a long narrow school and hired a teacher to run the school. Each school room had a door to the outside, like a mini strip mall. My family moved into the last school room. This was our apartment. My sister Liet and her family lived in the first school room. We had no extra money to pay rent for an apartment, so my aunt provided this housing for free. There was no water or electricity in our building. The creek behind our building served as our bathroom and our laundry.

My mom or sister would clean all of the classrooms each day. This was one way we could help my aunt and uncle for providing us with housing. It was very nice for them to give us a place to live, but it was very different than our bamboo house in Tam Ich. Many days I really, really missed our house and my life back in the village.

My mom continued to work after we moved to the city, but her business changed. She no longer had a stand outside our bamboo house. She didn't have to take the bus. My older sisters and mom pooled their money to buy a truck and hired a driver to drive the truck. He drove them to the mountain to buy bananas, coffee, ice, and other items to sell. My mom or one of my sisters would ride with him. In the school yard, my mom and sisters built a small store, and this was where she sold her items. Sometimes people would come over and request something special. My mom would go with the truck and get it for them.

I always wanted to ride in the truck. It seemed so adventurous. One night I crept out of the house and slept in the back of the truck. My mom and the driver didn't look in the back of the truck in the morning when they left, so I got to go along. They traveled to different far away cities. It was great, except for the trouble I got into for sneaking along in the truck. Back at home my sister didn't know where I was. I really scared her. When I got home, she yelled at me. She made me kneel down facing the corner for hours.

Once we got settled into our apartment, my mom and aunt arranged for me to take the entrance exam to see if I could get into public school. There was only one public school in Nha Trang, the Vo Tanh Public High School, and if I was accepted my schooling would be free. I was happy and my family was proud that I passed the test with ease. Everyone told me I was just like my dad, smart and nice. I was

Me, age eleven, in front of our Nha Trang apartment.

37

proud that I would get to go to the best school. Despite the fact that I didn't like school that much in the village, I was looking forward to attending my new school. Before I could attend school, I needed to get a new uniform, one that was appropriate for a public school student.

The blue and white in the uniforms of the flight attendants reminded me of those old school uniforms. Nearby, my birthday party friends were reading the magazine in the seat pocket. It showed a map of the routes flown by this airline, Northwest Orient Airlines. I leaned over and pointed to South Vietnam. The airline didn't fly there, but it was on the map. I wondered if they knew about the war I lived through. The thought of it made my head swirl. They say cats have nine lives. I think I must too.

12

NGUYET

Life in the city was entirely different than village life. I should have known that, I had visited the city before. It felt faster and more confusing. There was much for me to learn about getting around. I tried hard to make some new friends in the city, but I missed my friends from Tam Ich. Many of the kids my age were stealing, selling or taking drugs, I was surrounded with opportunities to get in trouble, but I managed to avoid them. My mom told me over and over again, "Trong be a good boy. Stay by good people. Stay away from bad people." It was like a tape constantly playing from her and into me.

In the city there were motorcycles, bicycles, buses, and cars—all sorts of movement, noise, and distractions. The buses were not as one might imagine. They weren't big and yellow with rows of padded seats. They were more similar to open bed trucks with a roof on them. They had only three wheels, one on the front and two on the back. The bus held about ten people. There was a small fee to ride on these buses, and the atmosphere was casual. The driver didn't really

My sister Nguyet.

monitor or restrict the amount of people. The driver usually had an assistant to help load people's packages and collect the fees. Anyone could sit in the front of the bus by the driver if you paid more money. If it was too crowded, people just waited for the next bus. Passengers jumped on or off even if the bus wasn't stopped. You could hold chickens, packages or children on your lap. If the bus was crowded, it was honorable to give your seat to the elderly, or to those with packages or young children.

In 1972 I was twelve years old. Nguyet, my closest sister in age, was fifteen years old. Nguyet and our older sister, Liet, were riding on a very crowded bus. Liet found a seat in the back. Nguyet was standing on the back ledge holding onto the pole as was common in overfilled buses. My sisters were wearing flimsy sandals, not shoes that could provide good traction if you needed to bear down and hang on. The bus went down a steep hill and didn't slow down. It just kept going faster as it made a sharp turn. Many people fell off of the bus, including Nguyet. Liet remembers more than ten people lying in the road. The brakes on the bus were not very good, making it difficult to slow down when going around sharp curves.

The bus driver had to concentrate to keep the bus from falling over and couldn't stop for quite a while. It was two miles or more before the bus could safely stop.

By the time Liet and others got back to the place where Nguyet had fallen, they realized Nguyet was in bad shape. She had hit her head on something in the road. She lay where she had fallen. There was a swarm of activity. Some of the injured were sitting up or rolling around, some not so injured were trying to help those more in need. Nguyet lay still. As soon as they could, they brought the injured people to a hospital. Long and Oanh were called to the hospital but there was nothing they could do. Nguyet left us that day and went to Thien Dang the beautiful resting place up high in the sky filled with angels, flowers, fruit, trees, and good people.

When I got home that day from school, I heard my sister was dead. This was the first time someone so close to me had died. I cried and cried; we all did. It was hard to accept that our sweet, quiet Nguyet had been taken from us. Thankfully Liet wasn't harmed! Liet was born in the year of the Dragon, the luckiest and most powerful of the Chinese signs. Perhaps her lucky dragon spirit protected her. Liet blamed herself for the accident. She wished Nguyet would have been sitting in the seat instead of holding on to the back of the bus. We talked about this over and over again. We told Liet it was not her fault. We were lucky she was with Nguyet, to comfort her, to get my family so quickly to the hospital, and to be able to tell us what happened.

In the days that followed we were immersed in the funeral process. We never had a funeral for my dad because we continued to pray for his survival. I had been to funerals in my village, and they were always sad but nothing like burying my sister. Nguyet was only three years older than I was. She was my closest playmate and friend. She watched out for me, loved me, and was with me most of my childhood.

Vietnamese funerals have their own customs. The dead are put in a simple coffin along with symbolic items of use in the future life, for example, paper replicas of shoes, food, jewelry, money or anything the family thinks a person might need to help on the journey. The coffin was sealed. A meal was prepared for everyone in the dead person's honor. The first plate was presented to the deceased on a table surrounded by lit candles. After some prayers, everyone joined in the feast.

My sister was buried in Tam Ich. The cemetery in Tam Ich was in a low area on the edge of town. It had no fancy gates, benches, or tombstones. It was a very humble resting spot, which was what we were used to. We prayed for Nguyet in the temple. It was a warm and sunny day, a day that should make a person smile and be happy. For us it was a gloomy day, and it was a day when I realized we would never move back to Tam Ich. Nha Trang was where we would stay. Many people attended the funeral, but I remember staying close to my grandma, my mom's mom. After our move to Nha Trang, we were further apart and saw her less often. On this sad day, I was attracted to the warmth in her. I could see the love and concern in her eyes for my mother, for her grandchildren and her great grandchildren.

My mother had good and bad days after my sister was buried, but her health and happiness never returned. It was a terrible time for my family. It seemed, almost instantly, on the day of Nguyet's death, another piece of my mother's heart broke and was never mended. It wasn't as if she was really sick, it was just as if she was sort of sick. For a woman only forty-two years old, she looked and acted like someone much older. As a boy, I wasn't very involved in my mother's care. My sisters brought her to a western doctor. I don't know for sure if they tried any Chinese medicine to help her, but I imagine they did. As hard as I looked, I could no longer find the familiar twinkle in her eyes.

13

U.S. WITHDRAWAL

My legs had been crossed too long and the bottom one was tingling. I excused myself, left my seat and made my way to the aisle of the plane. I walk up and down the aisle a few times, raising my arms over my head to stretch them out. I bent my neck from side to side and did a few knee bends. That felt better. I might as well visit the bathroom while I was up. The woman in the blue uniform was making coffee in the back of the plane. It smelled heavenly. Outside the windows it was dark—nothing to see but the lights on the wings of the plane. As I returned to my seat and buckled up, a child from somewhere behind me let out a piercing scream, and it all came back to me. The memories swarmed and haunted me as I sat frozen like a statue in Row 29, Seat E.

It was 1973, and I was in ninth grade, in public school for the first time. I tried to learn English in earnest. Ninth grade was quite the year. This was the year I became a teenager, and the year my brother got married and moved away. Oanh had given birth to her second child. Liet had a small child too. My mom was really showing signs of serious health problems. She was getting weaker and paler, it seemed, every time I looked at her.

Every now and then, Long and I would take the bus back to the village and hang out with my cousins for the weekend. They would take us shrimping in the night. We wore a light on our head and had a net. I wasn't very good at catching shrimp. They swam backwards to escape, and I was always moving my net in the wrong direction. My cousin could catch twenty shrimp to every one I caught. Those nights were a pleasant reprieve for me from the loneliness and sadness at home.

The war was in everyone's face. The political pressure to get U.S. troops out of my country was strong. American forces were starting to withdraw from Vietnam. Without the allied forces, the ARVN would not be able to protect South Vietnam. No one knew what it would be like if that happened, but we soon found out. Some of us lived through it. Many of us did not. Military losses were high. Fifty-thousand American soldiers did not return home. As for Vietnamese soldiers, more than one million soldiers (both sides included) died in the war.

Military losses are expected in a war. However, civilian losses were the highest. Two million South Vietnamese citizens and two million North Vietnamese citizens died in the war. A total of four million civilians were eliminated.

The death toll for Vietnamese citizens and soldiers combined was about twelve percent of the population. More than one out of every ten people died during the time I lived in Vietnam. If this war happened in the U.S. a twelve-percent loss would be similar to eliminating all of the people that lived in six states.

Of the citizens and soldiers that survived (North Vietnamese, South Vietnamese, and their allies), most of us were physically or mentally wounded and are still struggling today with these problems.

In 1972 to 1973 the U.S. forces started to pull out of Vietnam. The U.S. citizens did not want any more American casualties, the political pressure was too great, and the U.S. government responded by a withdrawal of troops and an end to U.S. support of the war.

Toward the end of U.S. involvement were some of the worst battles yet. Thousands of people were killed, both soldiers and civilians. By the time the U.S. was completely out of the war, the North Vietnamese were occupying part of South Vietnam. That year the U.S. made a policy to not allow troops back to help South Vietnam. It would now be only a matter of time until we lost our country.

In a secret agreement between nations, the communists were not to take over the country until a period of time had elapsed after

U.S. withdrawal of troops. This plan was devised so it would not look like the U.S. lost the war. The U.S. troops left my country in 1973. I mentioned that this was a bad year for me, but it wasn't as bad as 1974.

14

MY MOM

In 1974, Hoa and I were the only ones living with my mom. My mother was forty-three years old and very sick. She was trying Chinese medicine, even trying western medicine. Nothing was helping. We did not know what was wrong with her. Only that she was sick. We went to the temple and prayed for her health. We put tiger balm on her and tried anything we could think of. My sisters whispered about her when I was around. I did not know what to do, how to help her. I could do many things around the apartment to help, but I could not make her feel better. Sometimes I would take off and disappear for a while to escape the sickness and sadness of my home. As she grew weaker, my sisters and brother returned, and we took turns sitting by her and touching her and talking to her. Finally her body gave out, and she left us to join my sister Nguyet and the other angels in heaven. The elder said she died half of sickness and half of a broken heart.

The following days were filled with funeral preparations. My mom was buried next to Nguyet back in Tam Ich. Our family and friends surrounded us and made us feel less alone. The funeral gathering was healing to us. There was some comfort in being back in Tam Ich, our own village. We said our goodbyes and prayers and made offerings for her future life. One of the things we put in the coffin was a picture of my dad and my sister. We knew my mom and sister were already together, and we hoped that someday my mom's broken heart would be healed, the day when she could be with my dad again.

This was a difficult time for me. I was living in a war zone. The war was wearing on all of us. We all looked over our shoulders and jumped at the slightest noise. My older sisters and brother were off with their new families. I had lost my sister and both of my parents. I was fourteen, alone, and now I was the head of the family. I needed to take care of my younger sister. The immense feeling of responsibility hit me for the first time, accompanied by a feeling of despair. It was the first time I could admit to myself that I could no longer remember my dad. I didn't know my dad, except through the stories that others would tell. It presented a huge heartbreaking loss to me at a vulnerable age, the age when many Vietnamese boys without parents turned bad.

My sisters and aunt had told me not to tell grandma my mom died. They thought she was too old and were worried the news would kill her. Over the next few years, my grandma would ask about my mom every time she saw one of us. "Where is your mother?" We would just say she was working or she was busy or something. It would feel like a knife in our heart when this would happen. Eventually my grandma found out my mom had died. She understood we meant well by keeping the news from her, but she was filled with grief and sadness at the loss of her first-born child. She asked us many questions about the circumstances of her death and some days when I looked directly into her eyes I could almost see my mother.

15

OANH'S HOUSE

After I lost my mom, I was on my own with my younger sister, Hoa. Hoa was twelve and I was fourteen. Together it would be difficult to make it on our own. My savior, Oanh, insisted that we move in with her and her family. It was a relief to me that I would not have to be the sole provider. Despite my mom's long illness, she had managed still to take care of much of the everyday operations of our family.

Many things changed with the loss of my mother. Big and small things, things I never even thought about. Now when I needed a haircut, I had to ask my sister to cut it for me. My mom used to be in charge of this. I wondered if she'd taught my sister. Most households had a designated family barber. The first few haircuts were not so good, but with practice they got better and better. If you had some extra money, you could flag down the traveling barber. They would walk the city streets with a wooden box and a scissors. They would put the box down, and you would sit and get your hair cut, right in the street or in the park. If you had more money, you could go to the store where they specialized in hair cutting and styling. I never knew anyone that did this, but I

My sister Oanh and her husband, Tu Do.

saw the store as I biked through the streets of Nha Trang.

Oanh's husband worked for the ice factory, which was very cold inside. He brought heavy clothes, boots, and gloves with him to work each day. Most often he worked at the station where they stacked ice on pallets for shipping. He seemed to get sick more often than the rest of us. It probably wasn't good for him to be subjected to such a range of temperatures every day.

Oanh's apartment was near the ice plant and was provided at a much reduced rate for the employees of the company. The housing complex was a big metal building that many people lived in, all with separate quarters. It was like an apartment and a pole barn at the same time.

There were many young men, teenagers my age, in this building and we quickly made friends. One of the things we enjoyed was buying and fighting live crickets. We would each buy a few crickets, and we would pair them up two at a time for a fight. You would think, with a war on, we would have been sick of fighting, but for teenage boys it was a blast, and the crickets entertained us for hours.

My family shared several pedal bikes. There were always bikes scattered around the outside of our housing complex, and after school, friends would go out for a ride. We rarely had a destination. We were just out looking around, watching for soldiers and wasting time. If we were not in a hurry, we would make our way to the beach. It was one of the top tourist locations in the region, at least before the war. This region had a large stretch of the most beautiful ocean beaches I had ever seen. The beach wasn't far away, and we would go swimming and of course pay close attention to the pretty girls. I was shy, so I never talked to the girls. But in my mind it was a different story. I was no longer a boy, I was a man.

Shortly after Hoa and I moved in, Oanh's husband left the ice factory and took a job as a manager at the boat factory. It was a great opportunity for him to move from a laborer to a supervisor. Because of this, we had to move out of the company housing complex. It had only been a few months since my mother died and Hoa and I moved in with Oanh and her family. Now we moved again. Oanh and her husband bought a small house on the outskirts of town. It was located on the far side of the bridge entering Nha Trang. We were enrolled in a different school near the new house. I left my friends from the apartment without bothering to say goodbye. It seemed like I was a dragonfly, stopping to rest but not staying in any one location. This was my third house since I had moved to Nha Trang, my second home without my mother.

16

THE LANDING

The woman next to me nudged me gently. "Are you having a bad dream?" What was she saying? I looked at her and I could see in her eyes a look of concern. It took me a minute to remember where I was. I blinked my eyes, nodded and mumbled something to her. The flight attendant was heading our way with another round of refreshments. I gladly took a cool glass of water and drank it in three big gulps. As my eyes focused, I saw something white out of the window of the plane. I stared at it for a long time. What was all of this white I was seeing? Were we in the middle of a cloud? It seemed too far away for a cloud. I pointed out the window and, mostly in sign language, asked the women what was all of that white stuff below us? "SNOW." They repeated, "SNOW."

I had heard about snow. Snow was frozen fluffy rain and it occurred in really cold regions of the world. Polar bears and penguins lived in the snow. Children piled it in lumps to look like snowmen. It must be very cold where we were flying just then. Objects were getting easier to see out of the window. The plane must be getting lower in the sky. I was wearing my shorts, t-shirt and sandals, the ones I wore every day at the refugee camp in Hong Kong. They would be pretty useless in the snow. I knew the picture they showed me of Minnesota looked warm, with green grass, trees, and lakes. I was glad we were just flying over this cold place and not stopping. Minnesota would be warm, like Vietnam, I told myself as I felt the ice cubes in my empty cup through the thin layer of plastic.

My ears began to pop as the plane descended. People were rustling around, putting their belongings back in the bins and under the seats. The flight attendants were scurrying around picking up the last remaining coffee cups and napkins. A voice came over the speaker, but I didn't understand it. I watched the others to see what I should do. I was not sure, so I did nothing. I looked out the window, and it was still white. I was confused. Was there snow here? Was this Minnesota?

My heart started to pound from excitement and, well, probably nerves too. I was about to take my first steps in America, the land of the free, the land of opportunity, the place my sisters had told me about. The place I had barely been able to imagine. This might have been my luckiest day ever. I was living in a miracle. I heard my sister's words to me, "Trong, if anyone asks you where you want to go, say U.S.A., U.S.A., U.S.A."

A small cheer rose from the passengers as the wheels touched down. A loud voice came over the speaker. "Ladies and Gentleman, welcome to Minneapolis, Minnesota. The local time is 4:15 p.m. Please remain seated with your seatbelt fastened until we arrive at the gate and the seatbelt sign is turned off." It was April 15, 1980, exactly one year to the day since I arrived in Hong Kong.

Soon the seatbelt sign turned off, and people started to move. A line formed in the aisle. It was a while before it was my turn, but soon I was standing in the aisle, following the family In front of me down the long narrow path. I was carrying everything I owned in a small duffel bag. All of my money fit in one small corner of my pocket. My precious possessions were my memories, hopes, and dreams, the only things of value I owned.

PART II

TRANSITIONS

17

The Church

Prior to my arrival in Minnesota, the Messiah Lutheran Church in Minneapolis had assembled a group of twenty-one parishioners to form a refugee committee. The committee went into action in 1975 and bought a large house next to the church. They decorated, furnished, and supplied the house with all of the essential items a family would need to live . . . only families would not live there, just young men. In their research, the refuge committee found that most people in the United States and other countries wanted to sponsor families or children from the refugee camps. Most were leery of sponsoring single young men from such a war-torn country. They could be violent, wild or cause problems. This was exactly where the committee stepped up to help. They would take the young men. This would be their mission, their contribution to the world.

Jeanne Teigen was one of the members of the refugee committee. She was a single professional woman living in South Minneapolis where she lived with her mother. In 1975 when the committee brought the first of the young men to south Minneapolis, Jeanne was forty years old. Reflecting back, she says, "When they say life begins at forty, I now know what that means and they are right! What an adventure this was." Over the course of ten years, the church sponsored seventy-two people, sixty from Vietnam.

Jeanne had grown up an only child, with an absentee father, without any adult men in her immediate life. She found herself in charge of daily visits to check on the young male refugees, nick-named "the boys" by the church. She volunteered for this because it was on her route to work each day. She remembers the feelings she had the first day as she approached the driveway, thinking, *Dear Lord what have I gotten myself into.* She took a deep breath and proceeded. As she approached the driveway, she saw seven Asian heads all in row, sitting on the bank watching the cars drive down the road, as if watching a parade. She smiled and relaxed. From then on she was never nervous again.

The day I arrived in the United States was April 15, 1980, five years after the church sponsored its first refugees. On that April day, Jeanne took the day off of work and walked down the Red Concourse of the Minneapolis-St. Paul International Airport to Gate 23. She carried with her a sign that said TRONG VAN NGUYEN. My cousin Loc Nguyen, one of the first refugees sponsored by the church in 1975, told the Messiah Lutheran church about me. I knew Loc was in Minnesota before I left Vietnam. I wrote down his contact information. Later I was able to write to him and tell him that I ended up in the refugee camp in Hong Kong. I told him I would like to come to the United States. Loc was the one responsible for me being sponsored by the church. Today was going to be a great day, thanks to Loc and the church.

My Cousin Loc.

Jeanne Teigen, my American mom.

18

AMERICA

I stepped out of the airplane into a covered ramp. It was freezing cold in this small dark walkway, but I was only cold for a minute or two until I entered the Minneapolis-St. Paul International Airport. It was similar to the Hong Kong airport except, well except everyone was fair skinned. I mean they were white and tall. They were all wearing lots of clothes! Jeans, shoes, socks, sweaters, and jackets, and they all spoke English. I had never owned any shoes, socks, sweaters, or a warm jacket. My radio and the few articles of clothing in my duffel bag would not be enough.

There was an elbow-to-elbow steady stream of people leaving the plane. I took a few steps sideways to get out of the flow. I stood still in my sandals to look around. Was there someone here for me? How would I know? What should I do? They told me not to worry about it at my exit Interview at the refugee camp. They said the arrangements had been made. There would be someone at the gate to pick me up. Were they sure? What if something changed? Well at least I knew I was in Minneapolis-St. Paul, Minnesota, U.S.A.

Before I took my next breath, I saw, not ten feet away, a woman holding a sign over her head that said TRONG VAN NGUYEN. I could have wept from joy, but instead I raised my hands over my head and waved, hopped, skipped, and jumped towards her. She was smiling ear to ear, and so was I as we shook hands and hugged. It was very odd for me to shake hands with a woman, but it was explained to me that this was an American custom. We waited with a few other Americans until my cousins had deplaned, and we were all standing together. The Americans led us through the airport to the big glass doors of the EXIT. Just before we left the building, they pulled warm clothes out of their bags and handed them to us. Hanh, Thanh, and I looked at each other for clues, but, not knowing what else to do, we put it all on—hats, shoes, socks, coats, pants, gloves—and we left the building.

The cold air stung my face. It felt like the cold was traveling to my skin through the layers of clothes. There were mounds of snow on the edges of the parking lot. The snow was melting and running across the pavement in many places. The air was colder here than anywhere else I had ever been. It was forty-two degrees Fahrenheit. I was not used to seeing temperature reported as F, only C. I was confused as to what it meant, except I knew it was cold.

The sky was gray and it felt like rain or, maybe, snow. As I looked out the window of the van, in the areas where the snow had melted, I saw the vegetation was all brown. The grass looked dead and trampled. The trees had only branches, no leaves. How strange? Occasionally we passed green trees that looked like Christmas trees. They looked healthy enough. There were no palm or bamboo trees anywhere that I could see; no ocean either. Along the roadside there were some scattered cans and trash that looked like it had been there a long tlme. The Americans explained to us that this was the start of spring in Minnesota. Within the next month everything that looked so frozen would come to life and turn green and beautiful. I understood only some of what they said. I would never forget today—April 15, 1980—my first day in the United States.

19

MINNEAPOLIS

Jeanne drove the van to our new home in South Minneapolis. There were so many roads and buildings. We pulled up to a nice looking house, much larger than any I had ever lived in. My address would be 2511 Columbus Avenue, and there was a big bold 2511 fastened to the front of the house. We all got out of the van and piled into the house. It was startling to me this big house with the divided rooms. Back in Tam Ich, it was just open space inside of the house. We had no interior walls. How interesting and unusual to have all of these separate rooms.

There were a few young Vietnamese men already at our house; one was my Cousin Loc, Thanh and Hanh's older brother. I was very happy and relieved to see him. It made me feel more relaxed knowing I had other people who understood my language living with me.

The boys' house. Left to right: Thanh, Tai, me, Loc, and Hanh.

Jeanne waved for me to follow her, as she led me to my room. It was fantastic. The bed was so big and soft and fluffy. I wondered with whom I would have to share it. It had layers of soft cloths and blankets on it. Could a king have a better bed than this? Near the bed was a cabinet that, she pointed to my duffel bag, was for my belongings.

The next room she showed me was the bathroom, a western bathroom complete with indoor plumbing. There was a toilet, a sink, and a bathtub. This was the first place I would live with an indoor bathroom and running water. I had a strong urge to go over and try the tap to see how it worked. She showed me the kitchen, the stove, refrigerator, microwave, table, chairs, garbage can, plates, chopsticks, and a vast array of food. Most of what I saw in the kitchen was foreign to me. The plates, chopsticks, knives, pots, and vegetables looked normal, the rest a mystery. There were little yellow notes stuck on everything. They said, "table," "window," "door," "stove," "can opener," "sink," and so on. The only thing I saw that did not have a note stuck on it was the people. Jeanne explained to me that these notes would help me learn English quicker. I thought it was a great idea! If only my ninth grade teachers would have tried this.

When we completed the tour of the house and everyone had been sufficiently introduced, the Americans left. Jeanne, Mary, and Diane promised to return tomorrow. All seven of us simultaneously gave out a sigh of relief as we took over the kitchen. We spread out on the chairs, counters, and floor and talked in our own familiar language. Loc opened the refrigerator and took out a bottle of Coca Cola, and we drank a toast to our new country. We started to talk a little about ourselves, our families, and the predicament we now found ourselves in. Thanh took an errant sip of pop, and it went up his nose. As he was choking and sputtering around the kitchen, the rest of us started snickering. It really wasn't that funny, but soon we were laughing so hard we were gasping for breath. I think our pressure release valves had just opened up and we were unwinding. That gathering in the kitchen was the start of our own makeshift family.

I was tired. It has been an extremely long day for me, or had it been two days? I could feel my eyes starting to burn and droop. Loc suggested we go to bed. We got up and moved upstairs. I headed to my room and so did everyone else. We each had our own bedroom. It was nice to have my own bed, but even nicer to have someone who spoke my language right by me in the same house. I took off many layers of new clothes and crawled into the bed. This would be my first night sleeping in a western bed. At the age of nineteen, this was my first night sleeping in my own bedroom. The layers of blankets and sheets felt heavy against my scrawny body, and I sank into the softness of the bed. My head shifted around a bit, testing for a comfortable spot in the pillow, and while I was still offering prayers of thanks and prayers of safety for my family, I drifted off to sleep and drifted back to hell on earth, a place I frequently visit in my sleep.

HELL ON EARTH

For a few years, the war seemed quieter. The year 1974 was one of those years. Perhaps it was because I was caught up in my mother's sickness, moving in with my sister, making new friends and the like. I am not sure. But in 1975 when I was fifteen years old, the war came back with all its fury.

In 1975, North Vietnam started its final takeover of South Vietnam. The United States had officially withdrawn from the war, and, without our allies, the South army was no match for the North army and their communist allies of China and Russia. The North already had taken control of some of the northern cities in South Vietnam back in 1973, so they were perched and ready to move without much warning.

The North army started on the mountain and moved south until they took over Saigon City, the capitol of South Vietnam. On May 1, 1975, once the communists were in control, they declared victory and changed the name of Saigon to Ho Chi Minh City after the late communist leader, Ho Chi Minh. The entire siege was fast. Saigon was one of the southern most cities and one of their last targets. Nha Trang was north of Saigon, so they came through our city first.

When they started their move to take over the country, word traveled fast. We had heard news that they were on the offensive and that the bombing, shooting, fires, and killing would be like nothing we had seen so far. People all over were digging trenches and tunnels, surrounding and covering them with sandbags. These were the areas of safety, the bomb shelters for those quick enough to get to them.

I was fifteen years old when they attacked Nha Trang. The city was in pandemonium. People were running everywhere, trying to get into the trenches. So many people were in the trenches that the ones on the bottom were smothered and crushed by the ones on the top. There were not enough trenches, not nearly enough. The sounds of the explosions, the shells, the screams of terror and death haunt me as do the moans and cries of the wounded. Many watched as their families were destroyed. My city was consumed, eaten alive by the communists.

I was a young strong boy ,and I ran to the mountain, the safest place I could think of. I ran fast and long, the sweat pouring off of my body and my breath short and painful. I barely noticed my discomfort. I could have kept running forever. I ran over rocks and sticks, turning my ankles and scratching my body. I ran by myself, leaving behind my family and friends. From a rocky outcrop high on the mountain I watched.

I could see the planes, the bombs and guns, the soldiers in their khaki uniforms, their tanks and artillery. I could see the mortars drop from the sky. I could see the houses on fire. I could see people being killed and injured. I can still clearly hear their cries for help. It happened right in front of my eyes. The smell of burning people was in the air. It made me sick.

The South army tried to stop the advance of the North Vietnamese by bombing the bridge, but they missed and hit a small village—the village where we lived in our new house. Many people were killed, hurt, or their houses burned down. Our house was unharmed.

The North army was only in our city a few days before they conquered it and proceeded to a new battlefield south of us. It was during this time that I became a prisoner of war. The North army didn't take me prisoner, my mind did. It has burnt the smells, sights, sounds, and feelings of terror into the core of my brain, and I have never been able to escape from it. I return to this scene often and without warning, to remember and re-live in vivid detail the worst side of mankind.

21

NIGHTMARE

I felt someone's hands on my shoulders, and I screamed with all my might. My forehead was drenched in sweat, and all my blankets were in a tangle next to my bed. Loc was standing by my bed, gently shaking me. "It is okay," he said. "Wake up. It is only a dream." I sobbed and sobbed until no more tears came. He sat on my bed as I cried, and he told me it was okay, it was normal. Loc turned on the lamp by my bed so I could see where I was. Eventually I lay back down, exhausted. He pulled the covers over me and crawled back into his own bed. I lay in my bed the rest of the night with one eye open, looking at the lamp. I was afraid to fall asleep.

The next day I came downstairs, and a few of my housemates were sitting in the kitchen drinking tea and talking. Thanh was trying to read an American newspaper. They waved to me. I poured myself a glass of water and joined them around the table. All of our conversation was in Vietnamese. We talked about my bad night. They all nodded and told me I was not the only one. It happened to them too. I described a little about my nightmare as I filled up a bowl with rice from the stove. In between reading the paper and eating breakfast, they asked me what happened when I got back from the mountain. I began to tell them.

After the North Army left Nha Trang, I waited in the mountain another day before I dared descend and make my way back to the city. The city wasn't flattened except for the area where the South army destroyed the bridge in an effort to stop the communist advance.

Nha Trang seemed like a giant anthill to me, with people outside everywhere looking for missing people, transporting and burying the deceased, consoling others who were dying, and helping the injured

64

the best they could with the entire city essentially out of order. They were picking up pieces of the bridges, the houses, and the stores. The city was in motion, but with an impenetrable black cloud of sadness and horror over it. This process didn't seem to have an end, it just continued on day and night, and eventually it was our operating mode, our "normal" way of life.

After this attack, we were under communist control. Our flag changed from the familiar yellow flag with a group of three red stripes running horizontally across the middle of it, to a red flag with the yellow star in the middle. This flag made my blood run cold. It was horrible to me, just like the war, just like the communists. It flew over the city like a beacon of bad news.

22

MINNESOTA CLOTHES

The doorbell rang. It was Mary and Jeanne. I quickly darted upstairs to get dressed before they could see me. I found the bathroom and a towel and splashed some water on my face and hair. I looked longingly at the bathtub, promising myself soon I would fill it with water and soak in it. Someone's comb was sitting on the edge of the sink, and I quickly ran it through my hair. I put on the pants and sweatshirt Ms. Teigen gave me yesterday. I found my sandals near my bed and slipped them on. Then I straightened up the blankets on my bed before I headed downstairs.

By the time I got downstairs, everyone was in the living room. Jeanne greeted me and told me I could call her "mom" if I would like. The Vietnamese word for mother is "Ma." The American word is "mom." This was one of the first English words I learned in America. This was my American mom, Jeanne Teigen. Jeanne had with her many big sacks of clothes we carried in from her car. The three of us were going to get a set of our own warm Minesota clothes. The bags were filled with shoes, boots, and clothes of every type donated by the church. Jeanne helped us sort through the piles and pick out a selection that would fit each one of us. We put the extra clothes back into the big bags and returned them to Jeanne's car. No one wanted the pink sweatshirt with the rose on it, but it somehow ended up in our house. From then on we would laugh and tease about it and hide it under each other's pillow or in some other place hoping to embarrass the person who found it.

We all got into Jeanne's car, and she drove us over to her house. It was a very big house for just two people and one cat. We met her mom, and we all called her grandma. We now had a new American grandma. Jeanne showed us around the house and had us practice saying American words like, "couch," "TV," "rug." Most things were hard to pronounce but we gave it a good try.

It fascinated me to look around an American house. They were so different from our Vietnamese houses—many more rooms and so sturdy. Big glass windows, big refrigerators, fancy curtains, giant TVs, and little tables everywhere with trinkets on them. There were colorful, interesting and unusual things everywhere. I had no idea what they were used for. There were big stuffed chairs and couches and nothing, not a single thing, geared for sitting on the floor. Of all the rooms, the bathrooms were the most remarkable rooms of all to me. Such luxury and convenience. I couldn't wait to try it out . . . I hoped I could figure it all out.

Grandma had made a pot of her special soup, and we all crowded around the table to eat our first official American meal. No chopsticks, only spoons and knives. The soup was red with tomatoes, many vegetables, and little pieces of meat. There was hot bread and butter. And for dessert, something none of us were used to having with our meals, ice cream. Grandma had her own freezer, and we did too at our Columbus Avenue house. I wonder what my mother would think if she could see me now? Could she have imagined such a life?

Having a new American mom and grandma made me feel happy but disjointed. I was one person but with two moms in two countries and three grandmas in two countries. I needed to spend more time thinking about my real mom and dad. I was determined to lock into my mind the things they said and did, how they looked and smelled, and all the things they taught me.

23

THE TRUTH

I closed my eyes and covered my ears. From my safe Minneapolis bedroom, I concentrated on my life back in Vietnam. I thought back to
when I was a young man, a young man growing up without a father. I
thought of the stories I had heard about his abduction from our home. I
started to feel a familiar knot forming in my stomach. That was the feeling
I had when I thought about my cousin Ra.

When the communists took over South Vietnam, my cousin Ra,
the traitor, was not safe. Although he had at one time worked for the
Viet Cong, he had switched his alliance to the South army seven years
earlier. He had shown the South army the location of the communist
camp near my village, giving them the advantage for a sneak attack.
Now that the South army had disbanded, he was no longer protected,
and the NVA was looking for him. He was a fugitive from the law and
an outcast from his family.

When I was fifteen years old, I heard a rumor that he was back,
and I went looking for him. I was no longer a boy. I was a man, and I
wanted to know what happened to my father. I felt this might be my
last chance to ever find out. I wanted to find my cousin before the
North army did.

I took the bus back to Tam Ich. I went door to door looking
where I thought Ra might be. After a short one-hour search, I found
him. He was back in his old house, the house he had lived in as a
child. His family was not with him. He was the only one there. I stared
at him in surprise. I had hoped to find him, but I didn't really expect
to be successful so early in my search. He looked at me and waited. I

asked him what happened to my dad. He did not pretend to be innocent; he did not change the subject. This is what he told me . . .

"The communists knew your dad was a very powerful and respected man in the village. I was bragging, and I told them that I was related to Ca. They forced me to bring them to your dad. Once I brought them to him, they didn't need me anymore. My role was done, except to observe. The soldiers brought him in restraints to the mountain, isolated and outnumbered him so they could talk to him and intimidate him. They tried to convince him to switch allegiance, to join the Viet Cong. They knew he would be a good asset, a person who could tell the common people how good the communist are, and a person who could convince them. Your dad said no, never! He would not help them ruin South Vietnam. He wanted to go back to his family. I was in awe of such a strong man to stand up to the communists."

"After dinner he headed off to relieve himself, two Viet Cong accompanied him. When their backs were turned, your dad took off running. The guards caught him, but he broke free and kept running. He jumped in the river and started swimming. The guards took out their guns and shot him in the back. He was unable to escape. He died, and his body is gone, we left him in the river. Now you know the truth. Your dad is not coming back. I am deeply sorry for this. I am a worthless traitor to the family. Trong, you can kill me if you like. I deserve to die by the hands of Ca's son."

Just a short time after my dad was taken from us he was dead. All of those years we had held out hope for his return and now my dad and the hope of his return were both gone.

"Ra," I whispered, "but my dad was alive for a long time. You kept coming back and asking for money and for food for him, to help him."

Ra looked right through me. "No, Trong, he was dead. I needed the food and money for me and the others. I knew your aunt had money and that she and your mom would do anything to help your dad."

I had nothing more to say to my cousin. I did not even want to look at him, a weak and pathetic man. I left the village and headed back to Nha Trang. My heart was heavy with the news I would have to tell my sisters. My dad, my perfect dad, a great man, a real leader, was gone. He never swore, he never hit people, he had a special way of talking to people, and now he was really gone. I imagined my mom, dad, and Nguyet all together now up high above the sky. Maybe my mom was happy again. I thought I could hear her tune playing faintly, somewhere far away.

When I arrived home, Hoa and Oanh immediately looked to me for answers. Oanh looked in my eyes and read my mind. She came forward and gave me a hug. I told them the story. Oanh asked Hoa to watch the kids, and she set out on foot to tell my brother and sister. Hoa and I talked a little, an awkward talk between teenage brother and sister. Hoa was only one when my dad was abducted. She didn't remember ever seeing him. She had a wistful, sad look about her that made me uneasy. I left the house and wandered down the streets to find my friends. I wanted to be lost in the play of boys, not in the heavy thoughts of men.

The day after I returned from Tam Ich, I heard my cousin had killed himself. He drank the poison used for killing insects in the rice fields. The communists found him dead in his house. I didn't care about him; none of us attended his funeral. I was relieved that I made the trip back to my village in time to talk to Ra. I had helped my family learn the fate of my father. We could now close that chapter of my dad's life and put our minds to rest.

After Vietnam became a communist country, nothing was right. In fact we had no rights, no freedom. Our country suffered losses at all levels from the war. We lost twelve percent of the population, had many sick and wounded people, and many people with emotional problems. The infrastructure of the country was devastated. It was a time of chaos and restructuring. No one remotely associated with the South government had a chance of a normal life. People were looking for any means of escape to leave Vietnam. Nineteen seventy-five was the start of the mass exodus from Vietnam. Many people risked their lives and many lost their lives fleeing the country. The only real chance of escape was by boat, so people flocked in great numbers to anything that would float and here the horror stories multiply. Families already broken apart by the war were even further destroyed as family members escaped when they could, leaving others behind.

My teenage years from fifteen to nineteen should have been great years, the best years for most kids, playing high school sports, dating, getting their first jobs and planning for the future. For me everything seemed sideways. Nothing made sense. I had no parents, my country was destroyed, and I wasn't allowed in school. What should I do, whom could I even ask for advice? The song my mother hummed played on in my head for weeks at a time. So did her words, "Trong be a good boy, not a bad boy. Hang around with good boys, not bad boys." I knew this to be good advice, but it was hard to follow all the time. There didn't seem to be any good boys anymore. Sometimes I would travel back to the cemetery where my mother was buried just to talk things over with her and my dad.

I thought constantly about escaping from the communists or fighting against them. Fighting wasn't a good option now. They were too strong. Escape was very risky. I knew many people died trying to escape. The communists had killed my father, they wouldn't let me go to school, and they took everything from nice people. They had ruined my country. I really hated them. I hated them with every bone and muscle in my body.

During these mixed-up years, I couldn't find a real job. I should have been in school, but, after the communists took over, they required each prospective student to fill out a questionnaire about themselves and their parents. Because of my dad's affiliation with the South Vietnamese Government, I was not allowed to attend school at all. Without a high school diploma or any work experience, I had no real chance for employment. As the head of what remained of my family,

I needed work. Fortunately for me, my uncle was fairly wealthy by Vietnam standards and owned several buses. He was one of the drivers, and he hired me on as a helper. My main route was from Nha Trang to Ninh Hoa. We covered this distance several times each day. It was exciting at first, but as the months wore on, it became clear to me that it was a dead-end job, it held no future for me other than driving a bus. It was nothing at all like the career my dad had as a teacher. My duties were to collect money and lend a hand to people getting on and off the bus. I helped them with their cargo, washed, cleaned, fueled, and fixed the bus and did anything else that was needed. It wasn't great,but it gave me something to do, and I earned a small amount of money. There didn't seem to be any better jobs around. My whole life I had dreams of doing something else, something more exciting, something that would make my parents proud. I just had no way to get to that place, and I could feel my dream fading away.

Now that South Vietnam was gone and Vietnam was here to stay, there was no opportunity for me. As often as I would go to the government building and fill out papers to get back into school, it never changed. I was stuck.

One of our bus stops was at Ninh Hoa. Usually we headed right back to Nha Trang, but sometimes we would take a break there, in the middle of our route. This was where my grandma lived in a humble house next to a series of small square rice fields. She owned this house and the land. She harvested the rice and brought it to the factory where she paid for the rice to be cleaned and peeled. On her homestead, she also had a few orange trees, coconut trees, jack fruit, and many good things to eat. Nothing changed with my grandma and her tiny rice farm when the communist took over. It was too small of an operation for them to bother with. Her back was bent in half from all of the years she spent working in the rice fields. Many of the farmers and laborers were bent in half; they could not stand up straight anymore. I tried transplanting rice plants. My grandma taught me how to do this. It was very hard and tedious work. My grandma never complained about it. She just went to the rice field or the garden every sunny day and worked.

My brother Long, his wife and first two sons.

On those days when we had a long break, I would hang up my hammock and lay on it. I would eat a juicy, sun-ripened piece of fruit and swing in the hammock in the fresh breeze. I loved the time I spent on the farm. It was my favorite place. My grandparents never had much money. Farming was not a very profitable business. But that didn't matter to me. I loved it all.

My sisters and brother loved the farm too. Now that everyone had grown up, we didn't often come to the farm together, more often individually. By 1977, Oanh had five children, Liet also had five children, and Long had two. I don't know how anyone could raise babies in the midst of such an unpleasant situation. I hoped my nieces and nephews would have a better childhood than we did. So far it wasn't looking too promising.

Friendships ended, started and changed rapidly during the Vietnam War and in the time following the war. After the war, my brother Long found a job working at a small restaurant. Trinh, an outgoing young man about my age, was a customer in the restaurant, and they soon became friends. I also became friends with Trinh. Trinh had been a North Vietnamese soldier, and his parents still lived in Hanoi.

HONG

My life in Nha Trang was uninspiring until 1978. That must have been my lucky year, because I met a girl, and she was mighty fine! It all happened one day on the bus. This young woman with beautiful eyes was riding with her cousins to Nha Trang. I noticed her right away, and, despite being busy with all of the people, I found time to keep looking at her. I was glad I was wearing my new black wind coat.

It was the last run of the day, and my uncle was driving the bus. I was, as usual, his assistant. The bus was crammed with people, things were tied on the roof, all the seats were filled, and some were standing on the back. I was standing on the back too, which was where I often stood if the bus was crowded. It was a very dangerous place to be, a place where I was extra cautious, especially since my sister's death.

The bus was moving along, picking up speed. It was a cloudy day and a chilly ride with the afternoon wind blowing through the bus. Unexpectedly, there was a small explosion, and the bus jerked everyone around. It was a tire blow-out (maybe from too many people on the bus, I don't know for sure), but the bus started swerving, and people panicked. I told them not to jump. I held them on with my arms and my legs. Packages were shifting on the top, and things were falling into the road. I told them if they jumped, they'd be killed, and I hung on extra tight to the metal bars. I could feel my fingers slipping off of the bars as the bus continued to slow down. It took about one-half mile for the bus to finally stop. I did not fall off, no one jumped off, and we all were safe. My arms were burning from the effort of holding on so tight.

The packages tied to the top were all scattered and broken. Plastic bottles opened, and fish sauce was sprayed on the people in the seats. It was a smelly mess. The majority of the fish sauce landed on one person, the person sitting on the edge, the beautiful girl with the sparkly eyes. I felt sorry for her, and I offered her my new wind jacket. She was embarrassed but was happy to have my jacket to cover her wet and smelly clothes.

Everyone got off of the bus, and a few of the passengers helped us. It didn't take long. When it was ready to go, everyone piled back on, and we finished our route. In about three more stops, it was the pretty girl's turn to get off. She pointed to her house and said that was where she lived. She thanked me shyly for the use of my jacket. She said she would wash it, and I could stop by tomorrow to pick it up. That was all the encouragement I needed. She was so sweet and beautiful. In my imagination she even smelled nice, nothing like fish sauce. I stopped by the very next day after work. We introduced ourselves for the first time, Hong Tran and Trong Nguyen. She returned my jacket and visited with me just a little. I could tell she was happy to see me. When it was time to go, she invited me back again. I was glad she invited me back. I came back later that week, and soon we began dating. I owed it all to my black wind jacket and a lucky flat tire. Without that I might not have had a girlfriend at all.

Hong was good for me. I started smiling more, and for some reason started looking forward to the bus route each morning. She brought a new spark into my life, and created some of my nicest memories of Vietnam.

CONTACTING HOME

I was finally safe in the U.S.A. Many things have happened to me since I left Vietnam a full year ago. I must find a way to contact my family. They had no idea where I was, and I had no idea what had happened to them. My family had no telephone, so Loc suggested a telegram. I didn't know a thing about sending a telegram. He lent me five dollars and brought me to the Western Union Telegram Office. It was expensive to send a telegram; I had to pay for each word I send. I wrote in Vietnamese, but this was the English translation. "I am safe in U.S.A. at 2511 Columbus Avenue, Minneapolis, Minnesota USA 55417. Love Trong."

All I could do then was wait. I had heard it could take up to three months for a letter to get from the United States to Vietnam. Seventy-three days after I sent my telegram, I received a letter from Oanh.

Dear Trong,

Thank you for the telegram. We are so happy and thankful you are safe. We told everyone. We have been praying for you and thinking of you continually. We are all looking for a way to leave Vietnam except for Long. He wants to stay here. Liet is still running the store. Hoa has a serious boyfriend. He is nice, you will like him. We miss you very much but we are glad you are in the United States.

Hong has a new baby girl, your daughter, named Trang (pronounced "Tran"), was born in 1979. She is sweet and beautiful. She has the name you and Hong picked out for her. After you were gone a few days, Hong came to my house and asked what had happened to you. I told her you were gone, you had escaped Vietnam on a boat. I told her not to be angry with you, it was my plan, and you didn't know that you would be leaving Vietnam that night. She was so sad, she missed you greatly. Soon thereafter she came to my house to tell me she was pregnant, what should she do. I told her not to worry, we would help her. I stayed in touch with Hong. I helped her when she had her baby. Baby Trang stays with me some days when Hong goes to work. Trang reminds me of you Trong, she looks just like you. Hong is dating someone else now. He is good to her, and they are taking good care of Trang.

My eyes started to fill with tears and I couldn't see the handwriting. The letters danced across my eyes in a blur. That day I turned from a man into a father. I had a daughter living halfway across the world from me, a daughter who had never met her father. I was not a husband or even a boyfriend to Hong. I was a father who might never see his daughter. The tears ran down my cheeks but couldn't rinse away the new pain that had been put into my heart that day. I lost my father when I was three. My daughter lost me before she was born. I wondered when this would stop.

CONFUSED AND SUPRISED

Several things about America confused and amazed me. Figuring out which house was mine was one of my problems. They all looked so much the same. I was afraid I would walk into the wrong house. In Minnesota the doors were always closed, and the people stayed inside. That was so different from Vietnam. It was intimidating. I didn't want to make a mistake.

My cousin told me if I ever got lost and couldn't remember my house, to go downtown and stand by the big IDS building. He pointed to the skyline, the biggest building on the horizon. From there I was to call him, and he would come and get me. He had me write down our phone number and put it in my wallet. We laughed and joked about this. It seemed funny to both of us to lose your house and have to go stand by the giant building far away. Silly as it seemed, one day this happened to me—I couldn't find my house. As hard as I tried, I couldn't remember which one to go into. So, remembering Loc's advice, I walked and walked until I got to the IDS building. I stood by the big building and called Loc. I was relieved when he answered the phone after just two rings. Loc and the rest of them laughed at me. They didn't know I was lost. They saw me walk by just an hour earlier. In a few minutes Loc was there with his car and brought me home. This was the only time I lost my house.

Most mornings there was a newspaper of some sort on our kitchen table. We all tried to practice our English by reading bits and pieces of it. The contents of the newspaper continually surprised me. It was 1980, and it was a presidential election year. There were often cartoons making fun of President Carter or the upcoming presidential candidates. In Vietnam this would never happen. With communism you cannot speak or write freely. You would never see a picture in the newspaper of the president with a big nose or big teeth and make fun of him. It made me uncomfortable. I didn't want anyone making fun of the president of the United States. But I came to understand that this is a part of democracy and that democracy is very important.

One Saturday, Jeanne called and told Hanh that she was coming over and would bring us to the laundromat. Hanh didn't know what that meant, so we looked it up. All we could find was a reference to clothes. We guessed she was going to bring us out to buy new clothes. We all got cleaned and dressed up and were sitting in the living room watching TV when she arrived. She took one look at us and started laughing. "What's going on? Where are your dirty clothes?"

The boys and Jeanne. I am playing the guitar.

We looked at her puzzled. We thought we were going out shopping for clothes. We showed her how we looked it up in the dictionary, and together we figured out how we had mistranslated the meaning of "laundromat" to "clothes." We all had a good laugh over our mistake as we changed back into our everyday clothes, gathered up our dirty clothes and piled into Jeanne's car for our first trip to the laundromat.

The laundromat offered some challenges to me as a new American. It was hot and steamy. It was amazing for me to see row after row of large machines that people put their clothes in. The first machine washed them, the second machine dried them. I was expecting a third machine to wear them. It was so noisy and fast. It was nothing at all like the old days when my sisters would bring the wash to the river and clean it in the flowing water. It was nothing at all like I remember cleaning my clothes by swishing them around in a pail of water at the refugee camp. There were no branches or poles to drape them on to dry. It was automatic and instant, the American laundromat.

27

SOUTHWEST HIGH SCHOOL

The church committee enrolled me in Minneapolis Southwest High School. I had only been in America a few days, and already I was starting school. The American school was almost on break. The school year ended right around the first of June. It was already April, but Jeanne insisted we get started right away.

I was nervous on a number of accounts. First, my last day in school was when I was fifteen years old, almost four years ago. Second, in my last school everyone spoke Vietnamese. Third, I was told a yellow school bus would pick me up at the corner and drop me off. Other than that, I didn't know what to do.

The first day Jeanne took time off from her job at the Bureau of Indian Affairs and drove me to school. We met with the principal and got a list of classes. In this vast school, students changed rooms for each class. Jeanne, some school official, and I walked down the long hallways finding all the rooms and talking briefly with the teachers. They showed me my locker, a tall thin metal storage compartment for my books and jacket. It was labeled E-44. They show me how to open the lock and wrote down the combination for me. When all the paperwork was done, and after I had been given the tour, they dropped me off at an English-as-a-Second-Language (ESL) class. I was equipped with pencil, paper, backpack, locker combination, bus number, and a tiny notebook that contained my own address and house phone number, Jeanne's phone number at work and at home, the school's phone number, my schedule of classes, and my bus number. Jeanne said she would be at my home that afternoon to see that I got off of the bus okay. She gave me a wink and left.

I found an empty seat and took a look around. There were about a dozen students in the room, none of them in uniform. Several were Asian. Phew, maybe school wouldn't be so bad. The teacher said, "Hello, Mr. Trong Nguyen," and everyone took a turn saying, "Hello, Mr. Trong Nguyen," then their name and the country they came from. I grinned at the nice welcome and took my turn. "My name is Trong Van Nguyen, and I am from Vietnam." After the attention was back on the teacher, I couldn't help but repeat those words over and over in my head . . .

My name is Trong Van Nguyen and I am from Vietnam.

My name is Trong Van Nguyen and I am from Vietnam.

My name is Trong Van Nguyen and I am from Vietnam.

I started to hum ever so softly under my breath, and I began to relax. I was living in the United States of America, surrounded by thousands of non-Asian people. I had never been exposed to this, and it was difficult to get used to. I was used to looking like everyone else, blending into the crowd. Now I looked different, they looked different, everything looked different. My mind was a jumble, a mix of the old world and the new. It almost felt like I was two people in one body, happy and homesick.

I felt so blessed to be in Minnesota, a state that I had never heard of until just a few months ago. I felt so lucky to be sponsored by the church, to have been selected to leave the camp. I swallowed hard as I thought of my escape and all that I survived. I got a second chance. My future belonged to me. If I could concentrate, pay attention, and figure out how things worked over here maybe I could get my family rescued too.

Now that I was in school, Jeanne wanted to introduce me to the public library. I saw Jeanne's car pulling into the driveway. We were going to the library. I headed out of the door and waited for her. I opened the passenger door and got in the car. On the way over she told me that the library was free for everyone to use. It was filled with books and even some books written in Vietnamese. That would be nice. I would like things to read in my own language! The library was a brick building with its own parking lot. We went in the main door and headed to the front desk. This was where a person got a library card, Jeanne explained. "You will need this to check out books." She helped me fill out the form. Date of birth, July 26, 1960. "Oh," the man behind the counter said, "You're nineteen. So am I."

"No," I answered. "I am twenty."

Jeanne looked at me, nodded and explained, "Trong, in America you are nineteen because here you are born at zero years old. In Vietnam you are twenty because, when you're born, they say you are one year old. Really, you are the same age no matter where you live, but it is recognized differently depending on your country."

I looked at the man behind the counter, and he looked at me. We both looked at Jeanne, tilted our heads and in unison said . . . "Huh?"

I suspect I will always remember that day in the library when I found out I was one year younger than I thought. To this day, I pause when someone asks me how old I am. I still take a second to make sure I am counting in American years.

DRIVERS LICENSE

My cousin Loc had a driver's license and a car. That really impressed me. I wanted to drive too. Eventually Loc brought me to the License Bureau and arranged for me to take the written test. They handed me a cassette tape. The tape had the test questions in Vietnamese rather than English. I was able to pass the test easily given the Vietnamese questions. After passing the test, I was granted a permit and began practice driving with Loc. Driving was easy for me. I had done a lot of driving in Vietnam with my uncle's bus company. The traffic and the big roads in Minnesota were a challenge for me, but I adjusted to this. I went to take my driver's exam full of confidence, but I failed. I turned the wrong way down a one way street. I spent the next few months practicing, and then I took the test again and passed it with ease.

My first year at American high school was drawing to a close. My English was poor, but I was more comfortable speaking it. I didn't have the knack of speaking in English sentences, but I was getting better at knowing the words. I knew the words "book," "rice," "hello," "yes," "bathroom," "TV," and some new words, "hamburger" and "French fries."

My American mom took me and a few others out for dinner one night. She drove her car into the parking lot of the restaurant, but we didn't get out. Instead Jeanne rolled down her window and started talking to a big lit up sign. She said she was calling in our dinner order to the cook. We drove up close to the building and paid the restaurant owner through a window. We drove a little further and someone handed us several paper cups with pop and a big bag of food, all out of another window. Jeanne told us this was a drive through restaurant, McDonalds. She drove the car around the block to the city park, where we all got out and spread out our dinner on a picnic table.

I was completely amazed by the dinner in the bag—the hamburgers with ketchup, mustard, pickles, and onions wrapped in thin paper. And there were French fries in a big paper tub and pop in a giant cup. I could have shared this pop with all of my sisters it was so big. Yes! It was truly an American invention. I was in love. The hamburgers were so soft, the mustard and ketchup tangy and delicious, and the French fries hot, crispy and salty. I had heard about American hamburgers, but they never sounded good to me. Now I knew what they were talking about. It was so easy. I could give up rice, grocery shopping and cooking forever. If only I had some money. I needed a job!

EXODUS

In 1975 people started leaving Vietnam in hordes. Young men forced into the communist army were putting pieces of wood in their uniforms and using it for flotation as they tried to swim out of the country. People were building boats, pretending to be fishermen, but using their vessels to head to sea and escape across the ocean. Others were paying for a pass on any sort of sea faring vessel, any method of leaving the country. Thousands of people left Vietnam. Many did not survive. Those that survived have a story similar to mine.

The 9-11 attack on the World Trade Center reminded me of this exodus. The twin towers were going down, and people were jumping to escape, but most likely jumping to their death. The people in the buildings, much like the people living in Vietnam, were willing to take a small chance of surviving to leave their current situation. Both events were horrible for me and for many others. We still suffer from the shock of those events. Many of us find ourselves reliving those terrible days as if they were still happening, thirty years later.

The new government tried to stop the exodus of people. It was embarrassing to them that their own citizens did not want to live there. They would guard the coast and return any refugees back to Vietnam. Often placing them in a less pleasant situation than the one they tried to escape. To counteract this, the refugees would plan to leave during a storm, when the coast was less guarded, but that was the most dangerous time of all for overloaded and under-equipped vessels to take to sea.

Many of the escape boats were not seaworthy or were overcrowded. They often had no food or shelter, no life jackets, no navigation system. Some had no motors and no lights. Many believed that staying and living in Vietnam was a worse option than leaving and risking your life for a chance of a better existence. The process of getting on a boat and heading to sea was a quick one. If a boat was coming, it would load in the dark, in the storm, very quickly to avoid being spotted. You paid your money and rushed to get on the boat. Families were split, as only the fastest boarding a boat would get on and the slower ones would not. Mothers left with one child, leaving the father and the other children behind. Fathers would leave with children, leaving their mother behind.

There was no communication system between the boats and the families back in Vietnam. If the boat had a successful trip, eventually communication would be established, and families connected. But it took time, often years. For those boats lost at sea, no one knew what happened.

One day I was swimming in the ocean, and my friends and I saw something large and unusual floating in the water. As we swam out to investigate, we discovered they were bodies, floating toward shore, the horrible reality of an unsuccessful escape.

My uncle and his two boys escaped on a wooden boat. This boat had a motor but no tools or parts to fix the motor. Out at sea the engine died. The passengers had no lifejackets, no communication, and very little food, only what each person carried with them. In desperation they decided that the men would take turns holding on to the back of the boat and kicking in the water, pushing the boat across the ocean. My older cousin jumped in and tried to do this, but drowned. My younger cousin stayed on the boat and survived. Eventually the boat passengers were rescued and brought to a refugee camp. That is how we know the story.

If someone found a refugee boat, they were responsible to help guide it safely to shore. This was the law of the sea. Seeing a ship at sea was a wonderful sight for those crossing the ocean on a rickety wooden boat, a ticket to safety. For the lucky ones, it meant a journey with food and water to a refugee camp, most likely in Hong Kong or the Philippines. However, for the unlucky ones that encountered a ship from Russia, China, or an ally of the new communist Vietnam, it would mean a return to Vietnam and not a pleasant return at that.

One of my first cousins and his family had a shocking experience. They were in a small twenty-passenger wooden boat, about two days out at sea when a U.S. submarine emerged next to their boat. They had never heard of a submarine before. They could not believe this big thing was coming up from the ocean floor. They were extremely scared, but their fears soon turned to relief when the crew of the submarine took them aboard and rescued them from their boat. They got their first and undoubtedly last ride on a submarine. Not everyone can say that.

With the flood of Vietnamese refugees arriving, neighboring countries had to prepare to accept or reject the refugees. We came in a steady stream across the water for years, flooding nearby ports of entry. Refugee camps had to be constructed and staffed, and a system to catalog and track each person developed. It was a huge challenge. The camps had to be able to handle language barriers, physical and emotional sickness, birth and death. Relocating refugees was a global effort. The United States and Australia were two of the countries that accepted many Vietnamese refugees. The war was held in Vietnam, but the impacts of this war rippled across the world long after the fighting was over.

30

HOMESICK

Eighteen-year-old men are tough, flexible and resilient to most everything. Young men are like lions, out to stalk prey, or cougars battling for a territory, strong and fearless. Those years eighteen to twenty-one are dynamite years, years to look back on for most adults. For me those years forced me to break out of my old mold and form a new one . . . by sheer strength and will. Those were amazing and remarkable years of changing cultures and my way of life.

At the same time I was strong and resilient, but a part of me was like a new born baby. I'm not sure if I cried the first day I arrived in the United States or not, but it doesn't matter. My transition to life in America brought so many tears to my eyes, I thought I might drown. I cried every day because I was lonely and homesick, happy and scared. This lasted a long time, not days or weeks but for years.

As a new immigrant to Minnesota, I was quiet and withdrawn. Many days when I got home from school, I would lay in my bed, and the tears would slowly run down my cheeks.. My mom, Jeanne, said, "Trong, you need to get over it. You need to go out and talk, go out and be with people, be with friends."

I knew she was right. At first it was slow and difficult for me to make friends. My English skills were improving, but I was self-conscious of my looks and my ability to communicate in English. I tended to stay close to the Vietnamese people I knew and stayed away from the others.

None of us at the house especially liked cooking, nor were we any good at it. We did the best we could, but we spent a lot of time eating rice. The church had filled our shelves with food in cans. We were not used to eating canned food. It was so odd tasting. Some of it was really salty, some rubbery or mushy. The colors seemed odd too. Some days we would open cans and try to eat the contents. The fruit was probably the most similar to anything we were used, to but most of it was just too unusual for us. We were all raised on rice, fish, fresh fruit, and vegetables, water and tea, not much else.

Some of the men who had lived in our house before us introduced us to "house" restaurants. These were unofficial Minnesota restaurants in the homes of Vietnamese people. One could go there, and the woman would cook you a meal. You were expected to pay for the meal, but there wasn't a menu or a list of prices. I enjoyed these meals immensely. They were different than back home because the furniture looked so different, but the food tasted like I remembered. The cook and other customers were nice and welcoming. It was a safe, rejuvenating place for me and the others to frequent.

I am quite sure the health department didn't know about these home restaurants. They flourished when the flood of refugees entered the Twin Cities. Would the Minneapolis police care about all of the un-permitted restaurants? I hadn't encountered the local police yet. I wondered if they were anything like the Vietnamese Police.

THE POLICE

Back in Tam Ich there was a person I knew who now worked for the communist government. I spoke to him several times. He advised me how to apply for an entry level position in the Nha Trang Police Department and offered to be a reference for me. I was interested in working for the police because I thought I might be able to find some information about my father and where to find his body.

Shortly after I applied for the position, I was offered a part-time job with the police. My main duty was to go to the villages and run movies for them. We had no television or radio—the infrastructure of the country was in poor shape. This was one effort of the government to entertain the people. Many of the films were in German or in other languages, and I would narrate the movie in Vietnamese to those in attendance

One of my film assignments brought me to Hanoi over the Chinese New Year. I didn't know anyone in Hanoi, so my new North Vietnamese friend, Trinh, encouraged me to visit and stay with his parents for the New Year. I looked them up, and they welcomed me to stay with them. On the second day of the Chinese New Year, we received word that Trinh was very sick and was flown to the Hanoi Hospital. We all met him there. The doctors had no medication or equipment to save him. Trinh just lay on the bed looking at us. He was too sick to speak. None of us knew what to do but we tried to get the doctors to pay more attention to him. We couldn't just watch him lay there and die.

A desperate plan formed in my mind, I went back to their home and put on my police uniform. I took a deep breath and summoned up my courage. I marched back into the hospital and took charge. I kicked the chairs and tipped over the table and told the doctors they had better help Trinh or they would be in big trouble with the police. Somehow this intimidation worked, and they found ways to help Trinh. For three days we stayed in the hospital with him, and then I had to go back to my work. I could tell he was starting to feel a little better, but no one knew what was wrong or what the prognosis was. His family was sad to see me go. Trinh was too sick to know I was leaving. It seemed surreal to me that I had a new family that I was welcomed into and that family was from North Vietnam.

32

MOUNT SINAI HOSPITAL

I wanted a job! I wanted to make money. I wanted to become independent. I passed by Mount Sinai Hospital every day and admired how large it was. One day after school, I walked inside the hospital and ask them for a job. They gave me an application to complete. I brought it home with me, and with the help of some of the others at home, I filled it out. The next day I walked over and turned it in, hoping for a positive response. A few days later, I received a call—they wanted to meet with me. I was nervous but excited at the possibility of a job. After school, I reported to the hospital, and someone from the kitchen staff met with me and showed me around. They explained some of the work responsibilities and asked me a series of questions. My English was not very good, but it was good enough for them. They hired me that day. Work would start Monday after school. I was now a food aid at Mount Sinai hospital.

I worked full time in the summer, and I worked part time during the school year. Receiving my first paycheck was one of my proudest and happiest moments since I arrived in Minnesota. They gave me a check, my first check. I didn't even know what a check was. I never had seen one in Vietnam or Hong Kong. I brought it to Jeanne, and she helped me set up a bank account. I learn of how to deposit money and started to save. My family in Vietnam never had a bank account. My mom just wore the money in a flat purse under her clothes. We never got paid in checks back then. I wondered what she would think of this. With my first paycheck, I went to the store and bought a wallet. I was very proud to have a job, a wallet, some money and an account at the bank. I was beginning to be a part of America. I knew exactly what my next purchase would be. I looked for the closest McDonalds I could find.

The staff I worked with at Mount Sinai Hospital were wonderful. They were all Americans, and they were very good at teaching me English. Together we worked hard on preparing and delivering food, cleaning dishes, and improving my English. When I was quiet, they encouraged me to talk. They gently corrected my words and my pronunciation. They also congratulated me or gave me high fives when I said something correctly. They struggled with me, helped and encouraged me. This was a great time in my life. I was making money, making friends, feeling more comfortable about my English, and gaining confidence. I was becoming a self-sufficient Minnesotan.

Now that I had a job, I was never able to do homework at night. I was just too tired. After my shift, I ate at work and went home to bed. I forced myself to wake up early in the morning to do my homework.

I was working as many hours as I could, and my savings account was growing! I always filled in for someone else if they needed extra help. Everyone liked my good attitude and flexibility. When I was not at work I was careful about spending my money. I had a plan to use my savings to help my family back in Vietnam. I didn't know how to help them yet, but I was sure they would need help, and I was going to be ready for them. I was, after all, the second son of Ca, a leader, a respectable man, the one who looks after his family and his village. I was just like him, so I was told. I loved my dad, my family, and my girlfriend Hong.

I had been feeling run down lately, too much work and school and not enough rest. But I was in America. The trip here had been far too long and difficult for me to sit back and do nothing. Now was the time to take advantage of my opportunities, and to make up for all I've left behind.

GETTING SERIOUS

Hong was getting serious, serious about me! We had been dating for over a year now. I was eighteen years old and smitten with my first love. We were like little doves cooing at each other. It looked silly I'm sure, but we didn't care. We spent more and more time together and enjoyed every minute of it. It was a wonderful distraction for both of us from the awful situation of living in our beaten down country under communist rule.

Hong was living with her mom and sister in Ninh Hoa. Her dad was gone. He had been captured and put in jail for being a captain in the South army. He was a prisoner of war. Because of her father's position in the Army, Hong wasn't allowed to go to school. She just worked helping her mother make and sell soup from a cart. I began to spend more and more time with Hong and her family and less and less time at my sister's house in Nha Trang. I was much happier in Ninh Hoa. I could visit my grandmother's farm, and I could spend time with Hong. Hong and her family were so nice to me. They made me feel welcomed and special. I thought I could stay in Ninh Hoa forever with Hong. I had joy back in my life.

Back in Nha Trang, my baby sister, Hoa, was growing up. She was nearly sixteen now and didn't seem to mind my absence. Liet and Oanh stepped in for my mother and took good care of her. Long was busy working and providing for his wife and children. It seemed for the first time in a long while, my family was stable, settled and making the best of the situation we had been given.

My Sister Beckons

It was a cloudy day, the feeling of rain was everywhere—a day that threatened an evening storm. It was the monsoon season in Vietnam. I was at Hong's house when I got the message that Oanh wanted to see me. We didn't have telephones, so the best way to contact each other was in person. Oanh sent someone on the bus to get off on Hong's stop and find me. I was to come home immediately. Hong was at work when I got the word. I didn't leave a message for her because I figured I would be back soon enough.

It turned out my sister had other plans for me, plans that were bigger than I could have ever imagined. She had a ticket for an escape boat, and she told me I was going to leave the country that night. I was stunned. I couldn't think straight. Fortunately, I didn't need to think, I only needed to listen. I had to listen to my sister because she was deadly serious. "Trong," she said, "you have no future here. You need to get away. You must start a life separate of the Communists. I have saved up the money for your boat ride. It is paid and the boat leaves tonight. Your cousins Thanh and Hanh will be on the boat with you. Your cousin Loc is already in Minnesota. Here is his address. You must contact him as soon as you can."

We had to time our escape. The boat was to leave in the middle of the night. Everyone who paid to get on the boat had to arrive within a ten-minute window of the departure, not earlier or later. Too much time with people around would attract the attention of the coastal guards. We took a motorcycle through the dark streets to our shoreline location. The person my sister paid was greedy. He took all of the money anyone would give him. He stuffed all of us on the boat, way too many of us for safe travel.

Our trip across the stormy sea was in a wooden motor boat. It was about twenty-two feet long by nine feet wide, about the size of a U.S. bedroom. There was a small cover over part of the main deck. The lower deck had no windows. It housed the engine, the supplies and many, many, people. Our boat had no shelter, no bathrooms, and no lifejackets. We did have a captain. The greedy man took money from 271 people, and all of us were wedged into the boat. He wouldn't be riding with us. He did not care if we survived. He only cared how much money he could get. Wedged tightly into the boat, none of us could move. The weight of the load almost sank the boat. Fortunately, large bundles of bamboo had been fastened along the outsides of the boat, like pontoons, to help steady the narrow boat sitting so deep in the water. Once we were in, the sides of our escape boat were only inches above the water.

I have no pictures of my escape boat, but it was similar to these.

Amidst the darkness, thunder and strong winds, the boat headed out to sea. The crashing sound as the boat cut through the waves and the spray of salt water on all of us muffled the sounds of the sobs and kept us all frozen in terror as we headed into the night. Sometime later, the rain let loose, and we were washed from head to toe with salt water and rainwater. We were baptized by the elements into our new life at sea. It was April 1979.

My sister's last instructions to me were, "Trong, if anyone asks you where you want to go say, U.S.A., U.S.A., U.S.A." U.S.A., U.S.A., U.S.A pounded in my head over and over again. I saw my sister speak those words, but it was in a voice that wasn't hers. I knew from some strange quality in her voice, that this was the absolute truth and my only chance of escape.

35

Day One at Sea

The boat tossed and rocked in the ocean waves like a little grain of rice in a giant pool of water. Sometime in the night, the rain stopped and the sky cleared up. We were all scared and cold, but the body heat of the person next to me helped warm and assured me that I was not alone on this journey. The night sky was so dark black that the stars shown like fireballs in the sky. They burned so bright I felt as if I could reach out and touch them. I pretended they were my mom and dad looking down on me in the midst of the dark yet lit up night, hoping they were watching over me on this frightening journey. My precious Hong—I hoped she would see these same stars and forgive me for leaving her. What have I done?

With the first light of dawn, my spirits lifted as I silently celebrated surviving my first night at sea. The communists hadn't caught us and returned us to shore, we were now likely past the Vietnam border on our way to Hong Kong. Unlike many others whose escape was intercepted by a Soviet boat, we were still at sea. If you were returned by the communists to Vietnam, they would take your home, your possessions, and locked you up in jail for two or three years. Miraculously, we were still at sea, the vast breathtaking big blue sea.

I sensed that all of us would be calmer and more relaxed today since we had escaped capture. In the daylight I noticed that some people were wiggling and moving around and some people were very still. Many, many people were very seasick, some so sick they could not move at all. There was no space on the boat to lie down. The floor was wet from the waves crashing over the side of the boat. We took turns bailing out the water with whatever we could find. It was hard work that didn't go away, but I didn't mind. It distracted me and gave me something to do. It was an important job. The boat couldn't take on any more water or weight or it would sink. Because of our cramped quarters and soggy floor, the best place to lie down was stretched across the laps of other people. Some sick people where propped up or wedged in between the people next to them.

The bail water was a concoction of seawater, vomit, urine, feces, and tears. There was no bathroom aboard the boat. Even if there was, there would be no way to get to it in our extreme crowded conditions. The strong healthy people could go to the bathroom over the side of the boat but that was scary and risky too, none of us had lifejackets, and our wooden boat was so small compared to the strength of the sea. Our boat rode just about ten inches above the water, weighted down by too many passengers. The old people, sick people, or small children just threw up or went to the bathroom where they were. It was up to the rest of us to keep the boat floating and as clean as possible. It was where we were going to live or where we were going to die.

I was fortunate I didn't get seasick. I was very happy to find a few barrels of fresh water on the boat. It needed to be shared by everyone in the tiniest amounts. I tried my best to help the others, to bring them some water or help them move to get comfortable. Everyone helped each other the best they could.

By noon the sun was at full strength burning down on us. The salt taste was on my lips and on my skin. There was an invisible layer of salt over everything and everyone. There was no place to hide from the sun or the salt, except for the small covered area that was already overcrowded. The relentless sun burned us like crispy potato chips. The best thing to do was to ignore it. I had no more clothes to wear for protection, no sunscreen, or soothing aloe gel, no hat, no umbrella. It was uncomfortable for me, but it was worse for those who were seasick. They had headaches and stomach-aches and were dizzy, dehydrated, and getting overheated too.

The day stretched on it seemed for weeks. All of us strained our eyes looking for rescue boats. Our questionable boat stayed within eye sight of the shoreline in an effort to have calmer travels. Fear and worry, hopes and prayers continually played through our thoughts like an endless symphony. I would doze off but awake to find the same music playing and playing.

DAY TWO AT SEA

The bonds of friendship were being built from one end of the boat to the other. When I boarded the boat, I only knew my cousins. The rest were a group of strangers living together in the most stressful situation imaginable. Every hour seemed like a month. Kindness, sympathy, and fears were shared between us. Our life stories poured out of us like water from a fountain. This might be the end of the rope for all of us, and we all knew it. There was no reason to keep it inside. Already, I knew at least fifty people.

I found that if I kept busy, those thoughts of despair faded, instead of screaming like headlines. With the number of very sick and uncomfortable people, I could always find something to do, someone to talk to or help in some way.

I wasn't the only one helping others—other refugees helped me too. I didn't know enough to bring anything with me. I came aboard wearing my sandals, a t-shirt, and shorts. I brought no food, water, sunglasses, sunscreen, or extra clothes. I had nothing. Most of the passengers were smarter than I had been. They brought some food with them. As you can imagine, food and fresh water were extremely valuable to all of us. There was no new supply of either. Some of the people I helped would share a little food with me. I will never forget their generosity. The boat owners supplied some fresh water and dry food like crackers. Many of the passengers were too sick to eat, they only wanted water.

The smell from the boat was terrible. I took shallow breaths to try to avoid it. The hot sun made it worse. I hoped for a breeze to blow the smell away, but it surrounded me, forcing its way into my nose and mouth. It gagged me, and made me cry. It wasn't fair. My mind was filled with many questions. Why was my life such a struggle? What was happening to me? Was there a god above, or have I been abandoned? When would it end? I was alone and missed my family. Would I ever be allowed back in Vietnam? What would I do in another country? I had to get control of myself. I need to make a plan. I had to figure out a way to see my family again.

As miserable as I was, it was clear that others had it worse. The old man near the front of the boat was having a really rough time of it. He was sick before he boarded the boat, but at least he was accompanied by much of his family. They were working hard to make him comfortable, but he just didn't look good. Many people didn't look good, but there was something different about him. It worried me. None of us knew how long we would be at sea—another day, week or month—it was impossible to predict. We had all heard of many stories of people escaping from Vietnam, those who had made it to another land, those lost at sea, and those captured by the communists. Over the last three years since the government had changed, thousands of people had fled the borders. No two escape stories that made their way back to Vietnam were the same. We had no idea of what was in store for us.

37

Day Three at Sea

So far in our journey the ocean and the people aboard the boat were quiet at night. Only a handful of the passengers, the young men, were up and about. We would get together and talk in low voices. We would help the captain stay awake. We all looked at the compass to make sure it was on course. We studied it like a crystal ball looking for our future. We hoped fervently that it worked. In the dark we could see the lights of ships far in the distance. Our rescue, I thought, only they never came closer

Early in the morning on the third day of our trip, there was a stir in the front of the boat accompanied by loud noises and shuffling of people. The news traveled across the boat in a split second, the old man had died. His family cried and in the cramped boat tried to bow down to offer prayers. After a little while they gently lowered him overboard. It was the only practical thing to do in this situation, but it seemed insane. We could see him float and slowly bob and then sink down into the ocean depths. Our boat left him behind to finish his journey in this world and begin his journey into a better world. The unfairness of that day for the old man, his family, and all of us had changed us. The vision of the old man in the sea is imprinted on my mind and will never leave me.

Day Four at Sea

My lips tasted like salt. There was no way to get rid of that brine taste. My ears, shoulders, neck, and face were covered with blisters from the hot sun. Every time a drop of salt water touched me, it would sting. We bailed water continuously day and night. The dirty water splashed on us so often, we quit caring. I felt as if I was turning into a piece of leathery jerky, dried in the sun and covered in salt and slime.

The morale on board was subdued—no rescue boat, no new supplies. The wooden boat was filled with sea water and human waste. No land was in sight. It was only the compass that gave me hope that we really had a direction and that we were on course. People were weary and growing weaker from the prolonged seasickness and worry. Many people were hallucinating, seeing and hearing things that weren't there. I tried to keep a positive attitude and help out where I could. Helplessness radiated from the bodies of the sick passengers. Despair was clearly in the eyes of the young mothers. The deep worry for their children, their family's future, and the sadness of the separation between them and their kin did not need words. Sometime during the day I went below board and found myself a small glass of water. The highlight of the day was a handful of soggy crackers. They were delicious. I ate them slowly, savoring the taste of food and taking an edge off my serious hunger.

The day came and went, and darkness had settled in. The young were still moving about, but much of the boat was sleeping or resting their eyes. I'm not sure who saw it first or what we thought it might be but, we started to see light, speckles of light in the dark horizon.

As we stayed on course, the lights became larger and more distinct. They were bright lights, many lights. We had found Hong Kong. It must be Hong Kong with all of those lights. A ripple of excitement made its way through the boat, and everyone, even those who had been lying down sick, looked to see the lights. Hope was felt for the first time on this vessel as we saw land. With each minute that passed, the lights were getting closer. The weather that evening was spectacular with warm, clear skies and just a slight breeze. This was the weather that the cruise liners hope for, the temperate conditions for the tourists at sea.

We appreciated the calm weather, not for a luxury night at sea but for our survival. Large waves and gusts of wind would easily capsize our boat. After about three hours of heading toward the shore, a boat approached us. It was a police boat. The lights we saw were from the Island of Macau, a gambling island. The police informed us that Macau does not accept refuges. We could not land there. We could not believe those words, after losing one member already. Many of us were very sick and suffering from dehydration, heat stroke, hunger, and extreme anxiety. They told us no. They had to be able to see the overcrowded and extreme unsanitary conditions of our small wooden boat. They said no, we were not welcome.

Panic started to swell in our boat. We were so close, should we try to swim. Should we try to jump to the police boats? But before chaos erupted, we had good news. The police would escort us to a port in Hong Kong that accepted refugees. After about a one-hour delay as the police were making radio communications with Macau and Hong Kong, the police boats escorted us out into the blackness of the night sea. This time we were not alone. We had two guide boats to follow. It made me feel so much better. It was the first night on the boat that I slept at all.

39

FIFTH DAY AT SEA

In the sunrise hours of morning, we thought we saw land. It appeared and disappeared with the swells in the ocean. But it never totally went away. This must be Hong Kong. In mid morning our escort boat stopped and the police spoke to our captain. This was as far as they would proceed. They would turn back to Macau now, but they gave our captain instructions on how to proceed into port. As the land became clearer, our spirits soared. We could make it. We thought even the very sick would make it to land. There would be no more funerals at sea. No capture by the communist. We could see our saving shores of Hong Kong, the British Colony. We had spent our last night in the boat!

Towards the middle of the day, we entered the port. A Hong Kong police boat came out to meet our boat and guide us to a pier. We were tied to the pier but received bad news. We are not allowed to leave the boat. The paperwork in Hong Kong must be processed, and everyone on the boat accounted for before we could enter the refugee camp. This process might take several days. We were thrilled to be safe in port but dismayed to have to stay aboard our disgusting boat.

The police asked the captain to select a few people to come on shore and pick up food and water for our boat. I was one of the lucky ones. I jumped out of the boat on to the pier and almost fell down. My legs had turned into rubber and felt like they had no bones in them. The same thing happened to the three other young men. We looked ridiculous. How odd. With every step I took on land, it felt as if I were rocking and swaying at sea. We followed the police to a warehouse right on the shore. Here we were given water and food in big boxes to carry back to the boat. What a treasure!

Back at the boat, they started the process of counting us and recording all of our names. I imagined the refugee program had to figure out what to do with another boat full of people. From the looks of the pier, many rickety boats had landed here. Some were full of people, some empty. The excitement of the day died down eventually, and we settled in for another night in the wooden boat. This night was better and worse than the rest. Better because we were safe, worse because we knew we soon would be entering a new country, a new world and all we could do was to sit among the sewer and saltwater. We watched our sick boatmates as the night wore on.

40

SIXTH DAY IN HONG KONG

Whether I slept that night or not, I cannot clearly remember. But I remember how excited we were when the police escort came the next morning to take us ashore. I still remember the date, April 15, 1979. Those who were able followed the police to a large shower area. After the boat was less crowded, the sick and weak were helped off of the boat and brought to an area with medical assistance. I will never forget how good that shower felt. I was so smelly, sunburned and full of salt. The clean water ran over my head, and into my mouth and ears, and cleansed my body and my spirits.

All of our clothes were thrown away, and they gave each of us thong sandals, clothes, and a box of food. We were given medication for the large blisters and infected sores on our bodies. My dark skin was covered with blisters from the salt and sun. Some of the blisters had broken open in the shower, and the tender skin beneath was very painful. My lips and shoulders were blistered the worst. As we passed through the shower station, they directed our group to a warehouse nearby. Because of the heavy immigrant traffic through this port, they didn't have enough housing. We were temporarily housed in a warehouse nicknamed the "Black House." There were no beds or furniture in the warehouse, but we were all together, our entire boat. We were given mats and blankets, and we slept on the floor. It felt heavenly to me. I was thankful to be able to stretch out my arms and legs and lay down, to be still, not bouncing with every wave in the sea. I was clean, safe and not hungry. My legs still felt like rubber, but I didn't care. I had made it. *Da dum da* . . . my mother's tune played on and on in my head. It sounded loud and beautiful to me like it filled the entire room. My mother's tune comforted me as I grieved for my losses—my childhood, girlfriend, family, and country.

I was a survivor. I was one they would write about in the history books, one of the thousands who fled Vietnam in search of freedom. I had made it.

41

THE BLACK HOUSE

We lived in the "Black House" for about a month. It wasn't a very welcoming place, but we heard they were expanding their operations and building more housing for all the refugees flooding into Hong Kong. The Black House and yard were fenced, and they asked us to not leave the fenced area. We didn't mind, we didn't want to go anywhere. We were crowded and slightly uncomfortable, but we felt safe. The facility had its own bathrooms and showers, a nice change from the boat! Twice a day food was brought to us by truck already prepared. To reduce confusion, a few people from each group would meet the truck and bring the food back to our location.

During this month, many refugee boats arrived and more and more people were housed in the giant warehouse. Often I felt homesick and very alone. I would silently cry at night huddled under my blanket, wishing my girlfriend, brother, sisters, and I were all together in a better place.

When the new housing was ready, our whole group moved to the Kai Tak refugee camp. It was very close to the Black House, but it was a brand new, much nicer facility. Inside there were rows and rows of bunk beds three levels high. My bed was on the top. Thanh and Hanh slept below me. They gave us each a piece of plywood to put on the metal bed frame to sleep. Maybe it was because I was sleeping so high in the air, I don't know, but it was the coldest room I had ever slept in. The camp issued us photo badges with our names on them. Everyone had to have a badge to get in and out. At Kai Tak, everything became very official and efficient.

At this camp we received money instead of meals. Each day I would go to the camp office and get five Hong Kong dollars to pay for food. With this I could go into the city and buy what I wanted. The money didn't go far, but it went far enough to feed me. Most everyone liked this change because with this money we could choose to buy food more familiar to us. Along with the camp-issued money, lots of people brought money or jewelry with them on the boat. Maybe it was because of the money, maybe because of the war, who knows, but the terrible times most of us lived through started again. In the refugee camp there were frequent fights and occasional killings. Gangs of refugees would come and ask for money. If you didn't give it to them, they would hit or kill you. There was a great deal of fear of these newly formed gangs. It felt like we were still living in a war. My mom told me to be a good boy, associate with good people. I was afraid of the gangs, and I stayed as far away from them as I could. They never attacked me. I was lucky. Perhaps it was the lucky sign of the Rat that kept me safe

Once we were transitioned into our new quarters, one of my first outings was to the post office. I sent a letter to my cousin Loc in Minnesota telling him where I was and asking him to please help my cousins and I get to the U.S.A. Back in 1975, with the help of the Lutheran Church, Loc was sponsored by a Minneapolis church just as the communists took over Vietnam.

As I became more familiar with the camp, I discovered there was a wonderful program at the headquarters building that offered free English classes for the refuges. Attendance was voluntary. I went to every class I could. In class we only spoke English. Although my English skills were poor, they were improving, and I was waiting for the day when I could test out my new language in a new country. My dream was to live in the U.S.A.

Every month I went to the post office and sent a letter to Loc. I longed to send a letter to my family and girlfriend in Vietnam, to tell them I was safe and not to worry, but I didn't. A letter from someone who escaped communism could cause trouble. While I was living at the camp, I never received any letters or phone calls. I hoped and prayed to my God up there that my letters were getting to Loc. He was my only hope for getting to America.

42

THE RADIO FACTORY

The few refugees who knew English or Chinese in the Kai Tak refugee camp were able to find jobs. I wanted a job, but I only knew Vietnamese. Living in the refugee camp was boring and unproductive. Learning English was good, but I needed something more to do. I wanted to go to work and earn money. I was determined to get a job somehow. One of my friends at the camp spoke both Chinese and Vietnamese. He found a job at an electronics factory assembling radios. I didn't think they would hire me because of my language barrier, but one day I went with him anyway. My friend acted as an interpreter for me, and together we told them I would like to work on the assembly line. The factory representative hired me and put me to work near my friend. The understanding was that my friend would translate for me any instructions I needed and they would pay me at the end of the week in cash. I was thrilled!

My job was to put capacitors and resistors on one particular radio's internal board. I would position the small parts and a machine would solder them. I was a part of an assembly line. The job was very repetitive and dangerous. I had to pay close attention to avoid being burned by the solder. Since I couldn't speak directly to them, they didn't want to confuse me, and, as a result, they never gave me anything different to do. Each day I would do exactly the same thing over and over. I longed for something new and more challenging to do, but at the same time I was extremely thankful for having a job and having something constructive to focus on each day when I woke up.

Like many teen-agers I had been admiring the in-style clothes of the young people in Hong Kong. I wanted to be more like them. As soon as I had enough money saved, I went out and bought myself a pair of blue jeans and a T-shirt. Many nights after work we would wander into downtown Hong Kong for dinner. They had little wagons of food for sale scattered along the sidewalks and streets. Most of these vendors were not licensed and not allowed to be out selling their wares. The small bowls food was served, not in paper or plastic, but in regular china bowls. The vendors would wash and reuse them. One night I was eating a bowl of rice and fish. During my dinner the vendor took his cart and set off running. He just disappeared. I was left standing with his bowl and chopsticks, and I had not even paid him. It was the strangest thing. It wasn't until much later that I understood what happened. He was not licensed, and the police were out patrolling. I would have loved to tell my family about that funny experience, but during my time in the refugee camp I had no contact with my family back in Vietnam at all. I hoped they had a sense of peace that I was safe. I wondered if they were safe.

One rainy February afternoon, my friend and I were working on the assembly line. Suddenly my friend grabbed me and pushed me out of the assembly line and out of the factory. He escorted me to a small city park just outside the factory. He explained to me that the boss said the inspector was coming, and we both needed to disappear or we would lose our jobs. He explained that our company didn't pay taxes for us and would get in trouble if the inspector found us working. After a few hours of walking around and goofing off, he brought me back to work. I spent five months at the radio factory. I was lucky. Most refugees had no job. The people with no jobs had to stay in camp. That would have been awful. I was very thankful for my job and I worked up until my last day in Hong Kong.

MY INTERVIEW

D uring my days at the refugee camp, I filled out the stack of papers necessary to apply for immigration to the United States. Other than filling out paperwork and waiting, there was nothing I could do to speed up the process. One day I was told that the Lutheran church would be coming to Kai Tak and would like to interview me about the chance to immigrate to another country. I had never heard of a Lutheran church before, but I was very excited. I couldn't wait. I was anxious and hopeful that they would like me and choose me to be sponsored. I didn't sleep soundly for days on end thinking about my chance to meet with them. I remembered clearly my sister's words to me as I boarded the boat nearly a year ago. "Trong, if anyone asks you where you want to go say, 'U.S.A., U.S.A., U.S.A.'"

The day finally arrived, and I met with the woman from the Lutheran Church. She told me they were located in Minnesota. I didn't know where Minnesota was, but I knew it was in the U.S.A. and that was where Loc was living. She pulled out a map and pointed to the U.S.A. I remembered it from my school days. Then she showed me where Minnesota was located, in the very north central part of the United States. It bordered on Canada. The representative of the church showed me some photographs of Minnesota. They were beautiful, all with green grass and trees. She showed me a photo of a lake with people walking around it. She showed me photos of houses, and she showed me a photo of their church and a group of people, their refugee committee. This committee was responsible for her being in Hong Kong today.

Minnesota looked perfect to me. The only part that made me a little uncomfortable was that there were no Asian people in her pictures. I told her how much I wanted to move to Minnesota, that I was a good boy, that I hung out with good people, and that I helped people. I was not a gangster or a druggie. I told her a little of my family's story, of the sadness we went through and how I hoped to get a new start in a country without communists. I explained that I didn't know what a Lutheran church was, but that I was raised a Buddhist. Looking back, that might have been a mistake, but as it turned out it didn't matter. They just wanted to help me and the others get a better life. I think they hated the communists too.

It wasn't long after she left that I received word that I was to be sponsored by their church, and in April I would fly from Hong Kong to Minneapolis. I could barely breathe. I was speechless. The tears rolled down my cheeks that day in never-ending streams. I bowed down and offered prayers of thanks to my god up there. I sent prayers to my mom and dad and all the others killed in Vietnam that I was going to be safe. I was going to America. I was a lucky one. I was humbled at my good fortune.

Hong Kong friends. I am second from the left in front.

GOODBYE HONG KONG

It was 1980, and I could see the airport out of the window of the bus that I boarded at the refugee camp. I could see many low-flying planes with their lights flashing, circling to land. When I woke up that morning, I knew something great was going to happen to me. I had always been a survivor. I had the ability to take advantage of opportunities when they appeared. That was how I found out what happened to my dad. That was how I escaped from Vietnam. That was how I found a job in Hong Kong. That was how I would make a successful life for myself and my family. My mother was right . . .

The bus pulled up to the departing passenger level, and I got out at the Northwest Orient stop. I took my duffel bag down the two big bus steps and into the airport. I found my gate on the overhead screen. The escort I had from the camp was helping me with all of this. Four of us split off from the group and headed down the hallway to Gate 31. Yes this was right, Hong Kong to Minneapolis. In thirty-five minutes, the flight would be boarding. I found a seat with a good view of the gate. I didn't want to take any chances that I would miss my flight, the flight of a lifetime. I hummed a tune, a familiar tune, and waited.

The gate agent's voice boomed over the loud speaker, "At this time we will begin boarding flight 2 to Minneapolis Minnesota. All of those with small children or needing special assistance please come forward. Everyone else please remain where you are until your row number is called."

Thanh, understood enough English and pointed at the "29" on my boarding pass. It seemed forever until the gate agent said, "Ladies and gentleman. We are now boarding Rows 25 to 35. Passengers with those seat assignments please come to the boarding area."

The flight attendant checked my ticket and waved me ahead, I walked down the ramp and into the plane. It was a downhill walk, smooth and easy. I walked very slowly down the isle. The passenger behind me helped me to Row 29, Seat E. I remember thinking "I did it. I did it. I successfully escaped from Vietnam. I escaped communism. I can start to rebuild my life. When this plane touches the ground, I will be in a free country. I am a survivor! Oh, my god, I am a survivor!" Maybe I was superstitious, but the Rat had been a lucky sign for me. I offered a prayer of thanks, for all of the small and large things that had to happen, for me to survive.

PART III

AMERICA

As I write the third section of the book I am now nearly fifty years old. I am recalling my experiences in America, the rest of my life's story.

TURNING TWENTY

My first two years in America flew by as if in a whirlwind. I was living in a free country, surrounded by kind people who were trying to help me. I was never treated unfairly because I was Vietnamese, I never felt discriminated against. Jeanne and her mom were wonderful. The church was strong in support of its refugee program. Being in school gave me another opportunity to integrate into American life. The Vietnamese people I met formed a tight community, almost a miniature Vietnam. We started to get to know each other and look out for each other. I could feel my life turning around. I was learning how to breathe again. I could feel my strength and confidence returning.

During these years, I experienced every feeling from extreme joy to black sadness. Some days I couldn't believe how lucky I was to be living in America, eating at McDonalds or going to school. Other days I felt lonely and scared. It seemed that at age twenty I was a baby bird learning to fly all over again, like I just hatched out of the eggshell into a world of newness. I was adjusting to being a minority, living in a western culture surrounded by new people, and having the freedom to chart my own destiny.

My twentieth and twenty-first years were spent in high school and working at Mount Sinai Hospital. I was older than most of the students at Southwest High School. On my first day in American high school, I was nineteen years old, nearly twenty. I was smaller in size than most of the American students, and I was so far behind in English that it caused difficulties with most of my classes. I knew I had to study much more than the average student just to get passing grades.

I took "English as a Second Language (ESL)" the entire time I was in high school. My teachers couldn't speak Vietnamese, so it was up to me to learn English in order to communicate. My ESL classes really helped me.

I was very pleased with my job as a food aid at Mount Sinai. The work itself was nothing great, but I loved my co-workers. They were so friendly and happy to see me each day. The paycheck helped me become less dependent on the church and more self-sufficient. It was great for my self-esteem, and it fired my desire to earn money, save money and get ahead. I was thankful that the church refugee committee and members of the congregation were there for me and the others as we transitioned into American life.

Graduation

The day I graduated from high school was one of the best days in my life. It had been a goal of mine and of my parents. I would be the first graduate in our family. My dad, the teacher, instilled in me and in our family a respect for education. Ever since I was fifteen and banished from school, I doubted that I would ever have the chance to graduate from high school. When I was nineteen and starting American high school it seemed so difficult. I had wondered if I would ever be fluent enough in English to pass the standards at my school. Gradually it became easier, and then one day I realized it was going to happen. I was going to get a diploma. I was twenty-one years old the day I graduated. In two months I would be twenty-two.

Proudly I went through the commencement exercises, my cap and gown showing the Southwest High School colors. The band played "Pomp and Circumstance" to start and the school song at the end. It was a perfect day. I had my diploma firmly under my arm and hummed that familiar tune, not my mom's tune but the Southwest rouser as Jeanne and I walked through the early summer night, back to the car.

In the following days, some of my classmates had graduation parties. The first one I went to surprised me. The house had a big table filled with sandwiches, chips, salads, and a giant cake decorated in our school colors. It was unbelievable the celebrations that surrounded graduation. It was one more difference between the east and western cultures, or maybe the rich and the poor cultures. I liked it, every bit of it! It was great fun. I never thought for a minute about having a party of my own. Who would have organized it? Not the boys in our house. We were busy looking at cars and girls. "The boys" were not skilled at having a party with cake and sandwiches. Instead of a party, Jeanne, Loc, and I went to McDonalds to celebrate in our own American style. I cried many times on my graduation night. I cried tears of happiness. My dad would have been so proud of me. I was so proud of me. I know that I would have a good future.

Shortly after graduation, Loc told me he had a good job offer. He would be leaving us and would be moving to California. It seemed so far away . . .

47

ARMY OR COLLEGE

Sometime after the graduation parties settled down, I went over to visit my American mom and grandma. I told Jeanne that at Southwest they had a small career fair where the colleges, community colleges, trade schools, and the military had booths set up. I had gone to the U.S. Navy booth and signed up to be in the Navy. I wanted to go back to Vietnam and fight. I wanted to get even with those people who had killed my father. Jeanne said "absolutely not." The next day she marched me right over to the Navy recruiting office and cancelled my letter of interest. She made it very clear to me and the Navy recruiter that I would not be in the military.

She said, "Trong, you have had enough fighting in your life already. No more! You must find a better way to make a living. You need more schooling." A few days later she brought me to Dunwoody Institute. She thought I might like the mechanics or carpentry program, but I wasn't interested in those types of trades, I was more interested in computers and electronics. We got back in the car, and she drove me to Northwestern Electronics Institute (NEI). I liked what I saw and so did she. They offered me a small scholarship, and Jeanne signed me up for a two-year electronic technician program. The school also introduced me to student loans and helped me fill out the paperwork. My cloudy future was becoming more certain. I was going into electronics.

CHEVETTE

America had cars and trucks, the type dreams are made of. They were not like the old rickety buses I used to work on at Nha Trang. Not like the motorcycles or motor-scooters common in the city. They were fast, sexy, powerful vehicles. They were all around me. The cost of the really cool cars was beyond my means, but to own a car of any sort would be a dream come true. I worked hard and saved my money. I wanted my own transportation. I'd had my American driver's license for two years now and I was ready to be a car owner. I looked and looked, at magazines, ads on bulletin boards, and in the newspaper. Finally I found it, the car of my dreams. Well, maybe not the exact car of my dreams, but a car. I purchased a 1972 Chevrolet Chevette in the summer of 1981. I paid $700 for it. It was nine years old with 118,000 miles on it. It was bright red and had a stick shift and a cassette tape player. If you looked close you could see it was rusted around the wheel wells and had a dented side panel, but it was my pride and joy. I was a successful man. I owned my own car!

I had no indoor parking space and during the winter my car had trouble starting. Each night before I went to bed I would start it and let it run for about ten minutes to keep the engine as warm as possible for the long night. One morning I couldn't find my car keys anywhere. Finally I looked in the car. There they were in the ignition, after starting the car, I had come inside and fallen asleep. I had accidentally let the car run all night. In the morning I felt foolish. I had a cold car with no gas in it. It was not the best way to start my day, but I had to laugh at myself, for there was no one else to blame.

I drove the Chevette often. Many of the Vietnamese refugees in Minneapolis did not have a car. They depended on the bus or they just walked to their destination. I offered rides to many people, helping them get to doctor appointments, immigration appointments, or any sort of ride to help them get around town easier. I was always driving somewhere. It made me feel good to be useful and helpful to the other people. Some of the Vietnamese people I gave rides to I knew pretty well; some I had never met. The word got around that I had a car, and I was willing to help.

MOVING OUT

After graduation my life changed again. This time it was a pleasant change. I was working quite a lot at Mount Sinai and going to NEI. School was going well. I seemed to have a talent for the electronics class work. I was making friends, and my English was improving. I had heard enough from Vietnam to be able to keep up with my brother and sisters. My savings account was growing, and I was much more confident about getting around Minneapolis.

A group of us started looking for a house to rent. The group consisted of four new friends I had made, not the people I had been living with. I liked the guys from Columbus Avenue, my first American home, but they were not ready to move out. The church was bringing in more refugees, and they really needed all the space they could get in the "boys" house. It was time for me to stretch my wings and fly. The transition from Hong Kong to America was over, and I was ready to move on.

We found a nice house to rent in south Minneapolis not too far from where I was staying. It was big enough for all of us, and it was in our price range. The five of us would be living with and renting from one American man. We all had our own room and it was only seventy-five dollars per month per person.

I packed up my belongings, which had grown considerably from the day I first moved in, my one limp duffle bag in hand. Now I had my Chevette stuffed with gear, winter and summer clothes, my bike, stereo, record albums, books, and my most treasured possession, my high school diploma. I ran back up to my room and gave it a good blast of cleaning. It sparkled when I left just like it did on the day I arrived. I tucked the pink sweatshirt under the pillow as a welcome for the next family member of the "Boys House."

I made it a point to stop and thank mom and grandma for taking such good care of me. We were all happy on this day because it had worked. The refugee program had rescued me, and now I was able to fend for myself. It was a proud and satisfying moment for all of us.

BECKY

I was still quite shy and withdrawn in my twenties. Bit by bit I had opened up and made friends, but I still spent too much of my time alone. There was one exception, I loved little kids. I took every opportunity I had to be around them. They made me happy.

During an early winter blizzard, I saw an Asian woman with two small children at a bus stop. I felt sorry for them. I rolled down my window and asked them if they would like a ride. She gave me a quiet but abrupt "no." I asked where she was from, she said Vietnam. I smiled and started talking to her in Vietnamese. I asked where she was going. She was going home. She told me her address. They had a studio apartment very near my building. We were both so surprised that she lived so close by me that she agreed to the ride. Once everyone was safely in the car and we were on our way, I learned their names, Becky, Son and Lam. The two young boys took a liking to me right away but Becky didn't. I found out later she thought I was a show off with my good English-speaking skills and my car.

I wanted to be around the boys. I really liked them, and I sensed they liked me too. I could tell Becky didn't think much of me so I introduced Becky (her real name was Bichnguyet) to one of my roommates.

I often came along when they started seeing each other. My roommate went to visit her, I went to play with Son and Lam. It worked out great. Becky and my friend could have some time alone, and I would take the kids outside to play. We would play ball, hide-n-seek, and chase me. We would look at the trees, water puddles and squirrels running through the yard. We would often fill the backpack and go off on a little adventure.

Becky had a similar story to mine. She escaped from Cam Ranh Vietnam in 1980. Prior to her escape, she would go to the ocean every night with her two babies and walk up and down the shore waiting for an escape boat. Sometimes the communists would see her and question her. She would have to make up an excuse for what she was doing. Eventually her uncle's sailboat came, and she and the two young children escaped.

Her journey across the ocean was unbearably stressful. Instead of a wooden fishing boat, she escaped on a sailboat, a boat with no power backup. She left Vietnam holding a one-and-a-half-year-old and had her three-month-old baby tied to her body. The taxing conditions aboard her boat, combined with poor nutrition and dehydration caused her body to stop producing breast milk. Her milk was the only source of food for Lam. During the journey, Becky didn't get seasick, but many did. She had to take care of her sister and sister-in-law's sons because the women were so sick. Taking care of the two sick adults and four children required an enormous effort.

During the summer of 1980, Becky and the other refugees spent six days and five nights on the sea. For most of the journey the weather was temperate, but one night a big storm came up. A young man, a boy really, tried to control the sails, but they were too much for him. The strong winds grabbed the sail, and the boy fell overboard. Everyone was in a panic. There were no lights other than the stars. They couldn't find him in the ocean, it was too dark. The passengers couldn't save him. He was lost forever. The rest of the crew survived the storm and eventually ended up in the Philippine Islands on Palawan. Lam spent his first year of life in the refugee camp with his mother and older brother. In time, Becky's brother-in-law, who had already immigrated to Minnesota, worked with the United States Catholic Church to sponsor Becky and the boys and bring them safely from the refugee camp to Minnesota.

51

BECKY LIKES ME

The more time I spent with Becky, the more I liked her. She was a great person, with a kind heart. Her features and curves made my heart skip a beat. She was stunningly beautiful. Her eyes could look straight into my soul and understand my pain. She had a smile and a laugh that made my more serious face melt away, and she was becoming the center of my thoughts. I wondered about her husband, who I knew was still alive. What had happened to him? This was a subject she never talked about.

Becky had a hard time getting used to the Minnesota weather and the food. She was trying to raise the two boys, learn English, and adapt to the western culture. We talked a little now, and then but I mostly kept to myself. My roommate was dating Becky, so despite the fact that I liked her, I never told her so. I just stayed out of the way and played with the boys. The boys really liked me, and I really liked them. Playing with them gave me an escape from many of my thoughts and worries.

One day my roommate told me, "Trong, Becky likes you, not me. You should date her."

Becky had never said anything to me. I never said anything to Becky. But I was happy with the news, and I didn't waste any time. The next day I went to visit her and the boys. It wasn't long before we were inseparable. As Becky once told me, "I just followed my boys and fell in love with you too." I couldn't have been happier. I had a beautiful girlfriend with two beautiful boys.

52

LAM AND SON

Becky's youngest boy had no memories of life in Vietnam or their trip across the ocean. Son had some vague memories of his seven months in the refugee camp. At home we didn't converse in English, but with the strong influence of American TV and culture the boys picked up English fast, much faster than Vietnamese. We were happy the boys were learning English, but we were both worried that they would lose their native language. Becky told the kids

Lam Hoang and Son Hoang.

that they must speak Vietnamese at home. I remember many days where she would warn them to stop talking English and speak Vietnamese otherwise, "No food for you." I don't remember her ever taking the food away from the boys, but it was a good threat.

Often the kids would forget and slip into speaking English. Instead of scolding them, sometimes Becky would say, "I don't understand what you are saying." She would pretend she didn't understand English so they would speak more Vietnamese. Because of our interest and effort in keeping our native language alive, the boys learned to speak Vietnamese. Their Vietnamese reading and writing skills were poor because Vietnamese was not taught in school and neither of us had the time to spend with them to properly teach them the written Vietnamese language.

Lam and Son where growing into hardworking trustworthy people. They reminded me so much of Becky. They had pleasing personalities to go along with their smiles. Being minors under Becky's custody, both Son and Lam automatically became U.S. citizens when Becky became a citizen.

LIET'S FAMILY

For many, many years, people were looking for ways to leave Vietnam. In 1982, my sister Liet was happily married and had five daughters. The whole family tried to get on an escape boat, but Liet, hampered by the three younger girls, wasn't fast enough. Her husband and the two oldest girls got on the boat, while the rest of the family was left behind. My sister had no choice but to wait to hear if her husband and children made it safely across the ocean to a refugee camp somewhere. There was no chance for them to be together again unless the husband and girls would be sponsored by some organization and settled in another country. After that it would still be a long process for her husband to be able to sponsor Liet and the kids and reunite their family. For the time being, Liet could only pray for their safety and wait for news from beyond Vietnam. Trudging back to their house, Liet's world had drastically changed. She would have to live without three of the people she loved the most, her husband and two oldest daughters. In the midst of such great sadness she would have to figure out a way to support herself and the younger girls for what, at the very best, could be a wait of several years.

When I heard about this, I wanted to send money to help her. I didn't have much, but I sent her some money for rice, bananas, sweet potatoes, and corn. I bought lightweight jackets for my nieces and sent them to Vietnam. My heart ached for her and her family.

OUR DUPLEX

When I was twenty-three, Becky and I decided to rent a home together. We looked around and found a duplex in South Minneapolis we could afford. The duplex wasn't fancy, but it gave the boys their own bedroom, and we had a much nicer yard than the apartment. In 1984 Becky became pregnant with our first child. Combining all of our children, it would be our fourth, but our first child together, and the first to be born in the United States.

Don and Sandy were our landlords, and they were very good to us. At this time in our lives, we were really poor. I was going to school, and Becky was on welfare. We were good tenants. We didn't complain or cause any problems. Don and Sandy owned a lot of rental property, and many people who rented weren't careful with their property. They didn't take very good care of it. We kept our duplex clean, and we tried to fix things. They liked us, and we liked them. Don came to us one day and informed us he was lowering the rent. They must have seen what a financial struggle we were in and wanted to help out.

One summer evening when we returned home from a pick-up volleyball game at Lake Calhoun, we saw that something was wrong. The kitchen window was all smashed in, and glass was everywhere. Becky and the kids stayed in the car with the doors locked, and I went in to see what had happened. Our duplex had been broken into. Our old TV and radio were gone, everything was a mess, and the thieves took all of the meat in the freezer. We didn't really have any money or valuables, which I am sure they found out after searching the apartment. We didn't know what to do. I called Don and Sandy and told them about the break in. They asked us if we had insurance. At that time I didn't know anything about insurance, and even if I had, we had no money for that sort of thing.

That same week our wonderful landlords showed up with a used black-and-white TV and a $1,000 loan. We never asked them for anything; they just did it. We appreciated their thoughtfulness and made it a point to pay as much as we could towards our loan each month. We told our friends how nice they were, and we encouraged them to rent their duplex units so we could help them out too.

With the exception of the robbery, we have many good memories of the duplex. Our family grew and thrived there. One night I came home from work tired, my eyes sore from looking at those small electronic parts all day. Becky greeted me at the door smiling. Her eyes were twinkling in the way that I love. She walked me into the kitchen, a kid pulling on each of my legs. She had baked a cake, and there was a candle in the middle of it. The kids had made paper hats, which we all balanced on our heads, while the kids and Becky shouted out, "Happy Birthday!" It was a perfect end to a perfect day, my first birthday party.

55

OANH'S FAMILY

Four years after my escape, most of my family was still in Vietnam. Only Liet's husband and two daughters had escaped. My oldest sister, Oanh, her husband, and their six children wanted to leave Vietnam, to have a chance for a better life. In 1983 they had an opportunity to escape. In the dark of night, only her husband and one child were able to get on the boat. Oanh and the five other children did not make it.

Oanh's husband and child arrived in the Philippines. They were in the Philippine refugee camp for two years. I did the paperwork to sponsor them to come to Minnesota, and in 1985 they arrived. I was happy to have my brother-in-law and nephew safely here, but I was sad because my sister and the other children were not with them. Oanh had been like a mother to me growing up. I missed her and worried about her supporting five children all alone. I knew it would take a long time before we would be able to get the rest of them to Minnesota. I was determined that one day she would be with her family again.

56

BECKY GOES TO WORK

Becky and I were very poor, trying to make ends meet and trying to help our relatives immigrate to Minnesota. I was working, and Becky was at home with the boys and working odd jobs. She was also going to English-as-a-Second-Language classes that offered free childcare. After a few years, she had had enough. She wanted a real job with a real income. We both knew we could use the extra money.

I had many contacts with people working in Vietnamese restaurants, but Becky didn't want to work in a restaurant. To her credit, she went to the Lutheran church and met with a man who helped with job placement. He found her a job at Innovex Corporation in Hopkins. Her job involved looking through a microscope and working on IBM computer chips. She did very tiny wiring and soldering.

Her first day at work was difficult, not so much the work itself but communicating in English. She could read and write fairly well in English but had a hard time listening and understanding English. She also had a hard time speaking it. Because of the communication barrier, work was very stressful for her, yet she was determined to succeed. At home she practiced her English by watching TV, Channel 2, the children's educational channel. At work she carried a notebook and dictionary to help her communicate. She could understand what people said, but she didn't know how to reply. Since her English writing skills were better than her speaking skills, she would write down her response or questions in her notebook for her colleagues to read.

Becky was a great worker. She concentrated on her work and did a good job. She had a knack for remembering names and made a point of greeting everyone each day by name. Because of her overall friendliness and good work ethics, she was well liked amongst her co-workers. Her first supervisor, Gail, was excellent and encouraged her in her work. Together they spent months working on Becky's English communication skills. Her supervisor would speak very slowly and encourage Becky to speak English. She learned a lot from this company about electronics assembly, and after one year's time, she could speak English.

Becky still wears these bracelets every day.

Becky was so pleased when she came home with her first paycheck. We talked about how she should spend it, and I encouraged her to go out and buy herself some nice jewelry. You only have a first paycheck one time. Becky bought a set of beautiful narrow gold bracelets, similar to the ones the wealthy people in Vietnam would wear. She looked lovely wearing her new bracelets. To this day I still admire her and the bracelets every time she wears them. She makes me proud.

57

MY COUSIN'S BOAT TRIP

O ne of the young men in our Minneapolis house had survived a boat trip across the ocean much worse than mine. It was so awful that he rarely spoke of it, but we all knew that it haunted him. His journey started out much like mine, on an overcrowded wooden boat with a small motor. They were somewhere out in the middle of the ocean when the motor broke. They had no tools or spare parts to fix it, and, despite their many attempts, they could not get it running.

For days they hoped that another boat would come and help them fix their motor or assist them to land. No boats materialized. Day after day, the boatload of people bobbed and drifted in the ocean. Many people were sick and getting sicker. They had very little food or water aboard their vessel. After two weeks at sea, they had used up all of their provisions. There was no more food or water on board. No help was on the way, and they didn't know where they were. The feelings of despair were great and mounting. The heat of the sun and the lack of food and water were too much for the sick to fight off. People were slowly dying, one here, another days later. Everyone was hallucinating and in extreme danger from the hot sun and dehydration.

In order to save themselves from dehydration and starvation, the passengers on the boat were forced to eat the dead. The emotional trauma from this situation has never left the survivors. My cousin and his wife were two of the passengers. His wife was very sick and dying. She pleaded with my cousin to prevent the others from eating her when she died. I don't know what happened to her after she died. I don't want to know.

After more than a month at sea, the remaining passengers of the small boat were rescued and brought temporarily to a port near the China Border. All of the passengers required medical assistance due to their state of starvation, heat stroke, and dehydration. Only twenty-eight people survived that voyage. All of the survivors should have been given or should have sought out psychological assistance, but that wasn't provided and often not sought out. Many were ashamed of their own actions and didn't want to tell anyone about it.

My housemate went to Jeanne Tiegen one day and told her the story that lay heavy on his heart. He wanted to know what God would do to him for having to eat those people. With tears running down both of their faces, Jeanne assured him that our God is a loving God. He understood what happened. "He loves you more because of what you have been through. You do not need to worry. You are one of his children."

My friend was so relieved. He feared revenge from God for these terrible acts. He could not imagine that God would be able to love him after this terrible boat experience. Jeanne helped many of us deal with the emotional trauma in our lives. She was a mother and a mentor to many of us during this time of major transition.

CONTROL DATA CORPORATION

In the spring of 1984 almost exactly four years after I arrived in Minnesota, I was offered a job with Control Data Corporation (CDC). They came to NEI and interviewed me while I was finishing up my last semester of schoolwork. They told me I had a job with them as soon as I graduated. They would pay me a good wage, and give me health insurance and paid vacation. I had never heard of a more wonderful job offer. The pay would be three times more per hour than the pay I was earning at my part-time job at Mount Sinai hospital. What a stroke of luck for me and my family! I was so relieved and proud. My parents would have been proud of me too. This would be my first professional job.

My office building was large and impressive. I was an electronics technician. My job was to test the completed circuit board units. For each board tested, I would get a print-out of the diagnostics. If it failed, I would mark it and send it back to be fixed. If it passed, I would put it on the rack for shipping.

After I got settled into working at CDC, I felt like I could take on a part-time second job. My family both in America and in Vietnam needed the money. I saw an ad in the Domino's Pizza window, "Part-time drivers wanted," and I applied. I was hired and began shortly thereafter to work on Friday and Saturday nights. Most evenings when my shift was over, I would make a big pizza with all of my favorite toppings and bring it home for our family. Becky and the kids were excited. We would gather around our small garage-sale table and enjoy our late-night snack. After about three weeks of this, the kids said "No more, please, dad. No more pizza." I had to laugh. I never thought I would hear the kids refuse pizza.

My pizza-delivery career was a short one. At CDC we were very busy one week, working overtime to meet a deadline. I had to call Domino's and cancel my delivery shift for Friday night. That very Friday, the night I was supposed to work, one of our drivers was shot and killed for the twenty dollars cash he had on him. I don't know if that driver would have been me, but it scared me, and I resigned from my part-time job at Domino's soon after that.

59

MINNESOTA BABY

Tan Van Nguyen was born in 1985. He was our Minnesota baby. He was a quiet, contented baby and toddler. When we brought him to the babysitter's he would sit on the couch or the floor. He never wrote on the walls, acted wild or did bad things. As a child, he had asthma but as he grew older it went away. I quit smoking because of Tan's asthma. I stayed away from cigarettes for ten years, until the day of the fishing trip, this frustrating day when the fish weren't biting and the other guys were smoking in the boat. I couldn't resist, I started smoking again, but it would only be a few more years until I quit for good. Tan was the youngest one in our house and constantly surrounded by older kids who entertained him. They wanted him to be able to play along with them. For a quiet child, oddly enough, he was always the center of attention.

Becky and I raised our kids without a lot of money or possessions. As a family we had a pleasant life. It was important to us that the kids developed a good

Me with Becky and Tan.

147

work ethic, honesty, and respect for others. We had no patience for complaining or laziness. I told my kids the same thing my mother told me, "Stay around good people, stay away from bad people." I would explain to them what happened if you got in the wrong group of people, like the communists, the gangsters, or druggies. I had seen the worst side of people. I saw a woman's arm cut off one day in my village because she had a bracelet and ring on that two men on a motorcycle wanted. My children hadn't seen these things. It was up to Becky and me to try to protect them from heading down the wrong path.

60

Our House

In 1987 after living in the duplex for four years, we had finally saved enough money to make a down payment on our first house. Our new house was in South Minneapolis where we were most familiar. We were anxious to move into our own space, but at the same time

Our first house in Minneapolis.

we would miss our landlords, Sandy and Don. Over the years we had all become good friends.

As we packed up the rented U-haul truck with our possessions, I couldn't help but think back to my previous moves—my move from Vietnam to Hong Kong where I had nothing but the clothes on my back, the one from Hong Kong to Minnesota where I carried all of my possessions in a small duffel bag, and my move from the "Boy's House" to my own apartment where everything I owned fit into my Chevette with room to spare. Now we were moving five people—two adults, three children—and many things across town to our beautiful new house. Not a *new* house that we built, but a new house to us. As we were loading, I saw the volleyball and tennis racquets being carried to the truck. Many good memories were made on the tennis court and on the volleyball court, a free and fun source of entertainment for me during my twenties. Already the kids were old enough to play a little tennis without constantly chasing the ball across the neighborhood. It was starting to be fun to play tennis with them.

During my three years with CDC, I gained knowledge and confidence in my trade. I made many friends and had a chance to demonstrate my hard work ethic in a professional setting. It was good for me and my self-esteem. Days after we moved into our new home, Control Data had a large layoff, and I was without a job. I was in a panic. I loved my job and things had been going so well for all of us. Seagate had purchased the division of CDC where I worked, and they no longer needed us.

Losing my job was a heart stopper. I had a new house and no job. Fortunately Control Data helped us update our resumes and find new jobs. It was a wonderful service they gave to the displaced workforce. I quickly found a job as a technician at Maico, a company that manufactured hearing aids. I was very skilled at working on small electronic systems, and this job fit me perfectly. Maico was located nearby in Edina, Minnesota, and the transition from CDC to Maico was a smooth one. I have to thank CDC for the wonderful service they provided to help us find new jobs. I never missed a single paycheck.

61

SPEAKING AT CHURCH

Jeanne Teigen called me one day seven or eight years after I came to Minnesota. This wasn't unusual since we kept in touch over the years. She asked me to come to church with her on Sunday. This was an unusual request although at the time I didn't think a thing of it. The Lutheran church that sponsored us never pushed us to become Lutherans. I attended church services and church events occasionally but not on a regular basis. It was a very comfortable situation for all of us who were sponsored by the church.

That Sunday I put on my nice clothes and met her in the church entrance. She led me to a pew towards the back of the church. We sat in the back listening to the service, singing the hymns and just enjoying the presence of each other. I was half listening when I heard Pastor Erickson say, "Today we have a special guest, Mr. Trong Nguyen. Today Trong will share with us his story."

I looked at Jeanne and she nodded and gave me a little push out of the pew. As I walked to the front of the church, I was scared and sweating. I had never done any public speaking before. My mind was entirely blank. What would I say? Maybe I should run out the back door. When I reached the front of the church, the minister put his arm around me and whispered to me. "Trong, tell them your story. Tell them about life in Vietnam and your journey to Minnesota. Relax and tell your story from your heart."

I took a few more steps and found myself behind the podium. The microphone was on, and I could hear my own voice fill the church. I started talking about my father's capture, about my mom and my sister, about the war, about crying myself to sleep. My story spilled out over the next forty-five minutes. The church was completely silent. I was shaking as I lifted my head to look at the crowd. I could see their red eyes and the tears on their cheeks, the people in the audience were crying. The minister came up to me and took me in his arms. I walked to my seat with my mother's tune softly, silently, playing in my head as my racing heart started to slow down.

I remember hearing the closing words of the service and then the people crowded around me. They were hugging me and talking to me. I looked at Jeanne, she had tears in her eyes, but she was smiling. I smiled back at her. This was the first time I had told my story. It had been difficult for me but it felt like a tiny bit of my soul healed that day. I think my mom and dad were with me in the front of the church that day, holding my hand, giving me strength.

U.S. Citizen

When I first arrived in the United States I was issued a Green Card. This was my identification in America. It was my ticket to live and work in the United States.

I was not eligible to apply for U.S. citizenship until I had been in Minnesota five years. I did not start the application process until I had been in the U.S. seven years. Becoming a U.S. citizen was not a difficult decision for me. I loved South Vietnam, but it no longer existed. It may never exist again in my lifetime. I needed to be a part of the country where I lived. It was time to be an American citizen.

Jeanne helped me with the paperwork. She brought me the study materials so I could prepare for the test. The test had questions on it like: Who was the first president of the U.S.? How many senators are there? Who is a Minnesota senator? Who is the president of the United States? How many representatives are there? There were many more historical questions. I studied my U.S. history, and I studied the democratic system. In order to pass the test I had to be able to write in English. My English was good enough at this time, so that part didn't worry me.

One of my friends told me the story of an older Vietnamese woman who was being interviewed for citizenship. The judge asked her the name of a Minnesota senator. She said Dave Hamburger instead of Dave Durenberger. Everyone laughed except for the women being interviewed.

I felt prepared for my citizenship test, and I passed it on my first try. Both Jeanne and I were very happy. She told me I was smart. She might have been the first person to tell me that. I'm not sure but that day it made my heart sing.

It was a bright summer day when we went to the state fairgrounds for the swearing-in ceremony. We all stood for the Pledge of Allegiance. "I pledge allegiance to the flag, of the United States of America . . ." It sounded strong and bold. A blend of many accents all speaking in English honored the red, white, and blue, stars-and-stripes flag in the front of the stage. There were many people in the large outdoor stadium. When my name was called, I stepped forward to receive a certificate of citizenship and a small American flag.

When I left the fairgrounds that day, I was filled with pride for my new country. It was 1988, and I felt worthy to represent the United States of America. I was now a voting member of America, and I would vote every chance I got. I would vote for the right person. I never had the chance to vote in Vietnam. But while South Vietnam was still a free country, the people in my village elected my dad to be the mayor of Tam Ich. Voting is the voice of the people. It is a great responsibility in a free country.

Becky, Son, Lam, Tan, and me.

63

TRANG ESCAPES

M y daughter Trang lived in Vietnam until she was nine years old, In 1989 she escaped with her grandfather Dinh Tran to the Philippines. As was typical in our community, there wasn't enough money for the whole family to leave, so the majority of the family stayed in Vietnam.

At the time I was dating Hong, her father was imprisoned for being a captain in the South Army. He spent eight years as a prisoner of war (POW). During that period, Hong never saw her dad, and he never met his granddaughter. Unlike my dad, Hong's dad was eventually released and was able to spend time with his family again.

Grandpa Tran tried three times to escape. On the third time, he brought Trang with him. She brought them good luck, and the escape was successful. Trang's escape in 1989 was similar to mine eleven years earlier. She had to sneak down to the beach in the middle of the night. To get to the beach, she and her grandpa had to cut across the wooded steep mountainside and slide down the slope to the beach. One hundred and fifty-five passengers boarded their wooden fishing boat. Trang told me about her nerve-wracking and dangerous trip across the ocean.

Trang and Grandpa's boat left Vietnam and successfully landed in the Philippine Islands. From there they contacted me and told me their location. The first I had heard about their escape was the letter I received from them from the refugee camp. When I learned my daughter was living in a refugee camp in the Philippines, I was very worried and apprehensive. I had heard too many accounts of the officials taking the refugees from the boat in the Philippines or Thailand

and separating the men and the women and raping the women. My friend saw his wife being raped right in front of him. I prayed constantly that Trang would be safe and not harmed.

Since Trang was my daughter, a member of my immediate family, I was able to work with the church to sponsor her and Grandpa Tran. All of my family except my youngest son, Tan, had now lived in a refugee camp. Trang had by far the longest stay in the camp. Living in the refugee camp was much worse than living in Vietnam. It was almost like being a farm animal. The only good thing about the refugee camp was hope, hope for being sponsored and moving on to live in a free country.

The thought of my daughter living through some of the terrible things I experienced in my escape and life in the refugee camp tormented me. When Trang arrived in the Philippines, she was assigned a small room to share with fourteen people. It was a mix of people of every age and gender. There was no privacy. It was a privilege to get food and water. To eat, each person had to get in line and wait for food and water. Trang was strong. She thought the living conditions were much harder on the older people than the younger people.

In the camp, people were divided into zones, and each zone had a leader. The leader's job was to distribute to each family any information, materials, rules, or paperwork the group needed to learn about. Grandpa Tran was well respected in the camp, and after a few years he was elected the zone leader. Because Grandpa Tran was the leader, Trang and Grandpa were assigned their own small room. This made life was much easier for them.

Because of the huge number of refugees in the camps, the process of sponsoring Trang and Grandpa was extremely slow and backlogged. Right around the time Trang reached the Philippines, the Philippines quit accepting refugees because there was no more room. I wrote a letter to Senator Paul Wellstone asking for help for my daughter. During this period of time there was no guarantee for anyone to be relocated outside of the camp. The relocation wait at the time of

Trang's arrival was four to five years. After 1989, the year when Trang arrived in camp, they became very strict. Many people were not placed and were sent back to Vietnam. It was as if global security increased and the borders around the world tightened.

When I started the paperwork, I also started talking to Becky and the boys and writing to Trang, about how our family would change. We discussed many things. I wanted to make sure that Trang's arrival would be a happy one for our house, an arrival without hard feelings. When our new teenager Trang came to join us, our goal was that we all would love and respect each other. In 1991, two years after Trang's escape, we were granted permission to submit the paperwork. We submitted the sponsorship paperwork and waited for Trang and Grandpa Tran to come to the U.S.A.

Back in the Philippines, a two-camp system was operating. The first camp was where everyone started. This was where people stayed the longest. The second camp was just for those who had been sponsored. The lucky people were moved from the first to the second camp to wait the paperwork processing.

Every month or so, the zone leader made a round of announcements. He announced who would be moving from the first camp to second camp. For those sponsored, it was a time of rebirth and hope. This was an extremely emotional and trying time in the camp. Trang was elated when she received her sponsorship letter, but she felt really terrible for those left behind. After so long together, they were like family. The group had been through so much—the treacherous escape, crowded conditions, separation from family back in Vietnam, so many unknowns, and the very long wait for word on their future. Some people received devastating letters saying they were not sponsored, and that they would be returned to Vietnam. Trang still cries about life in the camp, and the heartbreak of the people who were sent back to Vietnam after such a long and difficult journey. I am deeply saddened for those people and saddened that my daughter should have had to be exposed to such difficult conditions.

The second camp was a holding area for refuges from Hong Kong, the Philippines, and Malaysia. In this new camp, Trang met a lot of people from Hong Kong. Trang told me that this camp had a better feeling. The people had a renewed sense of hope and excitement. Everyone knew they would make it to another country. Like the first camp, everyone was given food and shelter, but life just seemed better. Trang was in the second camp for slightly over one year.

Back in Minnesota, we were all looking forward to meeting Trang and Grandpa, but the process seemed to drag on forever. The waiting was so long, it gave us all an empty feeling, a sense of powerlessness. As we were waiting for Trang, many things were going on in our lives. We were now American citizens, and it was safe for us to return to Vietnam to see our families. It had been nearly fifteen years since we had been to our homeland. Becky and I wanted to go back to Vietnam for a visit. Lam and Son were not interested in going to Vietnam. Over the years we had saved up enough money. We arranged for Tan to be taken out of school to join us. Together we purchased our tickets and scheduled our time off work. We never knew when Trang might be sent to Minnesota. It could be days, months, or years. Our trip was planned for 1993, four years since Trang's escape. Unbelievable as it seems, a case of bad timing delayed our father-daughter reunion a little longer.

Me and Becky.

64

VISIT TO VIETNAM

As fate would have it, Becky, Tan, and I ended up in Vietnam the exact time Trang arrived in Minnesota. We learned of this just shortly before we departed. We had no way to contact Trang, nor did we want to delay her scheduled arrival. We arranged for a friend to meet Grandpa and Trang and bring them to our home to stay with the boys until we returned.

As Trang was preparing to fly to the U.S., the three of us boarded the plane and headed overseas. This would be Tan's first exposure to life in Vietnam, the country that formed and shaped both Becky and me.

We flew from Minneapolis to Los Angeles to Taipei Taiwan, to Ho Chi Minh City, Vietnam. It was about twenty-two hours of flying time. I was excited yet apprehensive. I didn't know what to expect or how the people would treat me after I escaped and left them there. Would they recognize me? I was very eager to see my brother, sisters, and the rest of my extended family. I wanted to meet the people important in Becky's life and see the places where she spent her youth. We both knew without saying a word that it would be an emotional time for us and a big change for Tan.

My oldest sister, Oanh, picked us up at the airport, and we headed back to Nha Trang, where I had lived and where my siblings still lived. It was a long eight-hour drive to traverse the 450 kilometers or about 300 miles. This was my first realization that I had changed since I living in the U.S.A. I had become accustomed to nice roads and fast driving. In Vietnam they drove slowly because the roads were narrow and full of potholes. Eventually we arrived at Oanh's house hot and jostled from our travels. We quickly forgot about that as we were greeted by Oanh's five youngest children who were no longer children at all. We settled in to an evening of lively chatter and storytelling. This was my first opportunity to meet some of my nieces and nephews. They were very happy to see me, and I was very happy to see everyone. It was also my first chance to introduce some of my family to Becky and Tan.

The day after our arrival, we went to see my brother Long. He lived nearby with his wife and five children. He was a bus driver, driving those unsafe buses very similar to the ones on my old route. The job market in Vietnam was very poor. The economy in general was terrible. They didn't have enough money to properly support a house of seven. Times were hard for them. When I embraced my brother and shook his hand, he kept looking at my arms and hands. He asked me which hand was my artificial hand. This confused me. Why was he talking about an artificial hand? He knew that I had not been wounded in the war. I assured him these were my real hands. Both Long and Oanh cried out when they heard this news. It was confusing to me that they were all excited about me not having an artificial hand. They explained in rushed sentences between tears and laughter that there had been a rumor here for many years that my hand was cut off because I was

My youngest sister, Hoa, and her husband.

stealing, that I had become a bad boy and that a gangster had cut off my hand. I shook my head, "No, no. I am a good man just like I always had been." That day we rejoiced in our family reunion and in the end of the rumor that had troubled them for years.

My baby sister Hoa, who was only a teenager when I left, was now a grown woman. She was beautiful. Seeing her for the first time as a woman, she reminded me of my mother. Hoa worked for one of the Chinese doctors who formulated herbal and natural remedies. Hoa helped him gather, dry, and prepare the plants. Her husband had a job building wooden boats. Together they had four children, two sons, and two daughters.

Our five-week visit went by very fast. We saw many of our family members and had a good time catching up on the news. We took the buses, the same ones that I used to work on to visit Becky's uncle. He was a coffee farmer. It was nice to meet him and to learn more about Becky's family. We toured my old bus route and stopped in to see Hong. How ironic that we were together again in Vietnam while our daughter was waiting for me at my house in Minneapolis. Hong and I had never both been in the same room with our daughter. Despite the empty feeling of not having Trang at this reunion, it was wonderful to see Hong and her family again. I introduced them to Becky and Tan. We sat outside, drank tea and caught up on the events of the last fifteen years.

Later that night at Oanh's house, I asked my sisters about the people in Tam Ich, I wanted to know how our friends and neighbors were doing. They told me how poor they were and how hard they work for little or nothing. We decided we should do something to help them. There were no telephones in Tam Ich in 1993, so all communications with the village were in person. I asked my brother if he would go see the mayor and find out how many families were living in Tam Ich. Two days later Long returned to Nha Trang and we started on our plan.

The first step was a visit to my Aunt's rice factory. Becky and I bought rice for all of the families in Tam Ich. For families of three or fewer, we would donate ten pounds of rice, for larger families twenty pounds of rice. It took us one day and two evenings to package the rice into ten- and twenty-pound bags. When the job was completed, we loaded our rental truck, and Becky, Tan and I drove the truck to the village. The mayor met us at the Tam Ich school, and he sent word for everyone to come and get the rice. When the people had all arrived, the mayor called off the father's name, the traditional head of the house, and he came to the truck where Becky and I gave him their rice.

When I handed the rice to them, they looked at me like I must be rich, like a king. The people were very appreciative and happy for their gift of rice. This had never happened before in my village. It was a reunion celebration! For one day the problems caused by war and poverty were forgotten. For one day everyone was happy. We were happy too, very happy we could help.

We traveled through the third-world country with our little American boy, Tan. He was a shy seven year old, being introduced to a world he had only heard about. Many people wanted to practice their English with him, but he had a very hard time understanding their English because most had a heavy Vietnamese accent. Tan didn't do a lot of talking, but he played well with the other kids. He brought a backpack of toys with him on the airplane. After dinner the neighborhood kids would show up. He would take out the toys and spread them around the room so everyone could easily play with his toys. The kids all spoke Vietnamese, and so did Tan, so he blended easily into the play group. At bedtime, the kids went home, and he put everything neatly away in his backpack.

Tan had never slept in an open-air house before. His bed for this trip was the traditional bed with a grass mat and mosquito netting around it. Young Tan didn't know enough to keep his body away from the netting and away from the bugs. One morning he woke up with mosquito bites all over his cheek. We shook our heads, we didn't even think about the fact that our youngest wouldn't know enough to sleep in the middle of the netting.

A few days before it was time to head back home, Tan approached us with an idea. On the last night that the kids came over to play, each kid could pick a favorite toy to bring home with them. The Vietnamese children must have had a similar idea because on the last day most of his friends gifted him a small toy from Vietnam. Those toys weren't as sturdy as the U.S. toys. They were soft and made out of a material similar to a candle. Tan wasn't used to this type of toy, and he quickly broke many of them. On the drive to the airport he was looking for, but didn't see any of his new friends. On the airplane he started crying. We asked him what was wrong, and he said in the saddest little voice that he missed his friends.

While in Vietnam with our youngest son, a friend of ours kept an eye on our other children, Lam, Son, and Trang. We were able to call home from Vietnam and talk to Trang and reassure her we would be there soon.

When we returned to Minnesota, Tan's second-grade teacher put him in English-as-a-Second-Language class. Tan had forgotten how to read, write, listen, and speak in English. Five weeks immersed in Vietnam had really changed his communication patterns. What was most interesting about all of this was that in the two previous years of grade school, Tan had no problems with English. It didn't take long for Tan to remember his English skills, but his change in language surprised all of us.

65

Trang Comes to the USA

Our father-daughter reunion was delayed two weeks, but it didn't lessen the thrill of seeing each other for the first time. It was wonderful. I remember looking at Trang, and holding her melted my heart. I hugged her for the longest time and picked her up and twirled her around. We were both in tears and smiles for days. That we never met each other until she was fourteen years old was, to me, another of the many unforgettable side effects of the war.

Trang's Vietnamese was perfect, but her English was rough, limited to commonly used phrases. It reminded me of my English skills when I first arrived. Becky, the boys, and I introduced Trang to the U.S.A. in many ways. We

Becky, me, Trang, and little Tan.

enjoyed the opportunity to show her around her new country, state, and city. Everything was so big—the supermarket, the clothes stores. It amazed and at times overwhelmed her. We bought her winter clothes. She had her own room. Her world was changing much the same as mine had fifteen years earlier.

Bringing the four kids together was the melding of two cultures. The boys were brought up in America, and the girl in Vietnam. They all looked alike, but their life experiences were vastly different. Once Grandpa and Trang moved in, our house seemed small. As soon as we knew Trang was adjusting to us, we rented a nearby apartment for Grandpa Tran. We helped get him set up and watched over him as he adjusted to American life. After he lived there a little while, he enrolled at the local technical college and got an Associates' degree in mechanics. He went on to get a job as a mechanic technician.

Despite being raised in different worlds, the kids got along very well. The boys would take care of Trang and give her American teenager tips. One day she asked the boys to explain what "cool" meant. She had seen it on a billboard and didn't understand its meaning. She was fast at picking up the traditional English as taught in the school, but the slang was more difficult. The boys had rough Vietnamese language skills, so it took awhile for the four of them explain and understand what "cool" meant.

The American school system was a big change for Trang. She started out in Sanford Middle School, a part of the Minneapolis school system. The Minneapolis school system was big and lavish compared to the Vietnamese or refugee camp schools Trang had attended. English wasn't spoken in her schools, but she had tried to pick up English in the Philippines from talking to the people in camp. She was able to pick up phrases like, "hello, how are you?" "good morning," and the like.

At Sanford we immediately enrolled Trang in ESL. She was an excellent student and already excelled in math and science. Unlike me, even while she was learning English, she got straight A's. School to her had always been a luxury, and she kept that attitude when she came to America. She took advantage of her opportunity to go to school and never missed a day. Trang wanted to be the best in everything. In Vietnam she had been the number-one student, and that was what she wanted for herself in America. For the first year of middle school, the English language intimidated her. I remember her telling me about a black kid who picked on her in history class. She was so frustrated, not because he was picking on her, but because she couldn't find the English words to talk to him.

During the summer, my company, Versa Electronics, occasionally needed extra unskilled help. My boss, Ed Wood, agreed to hire Son, Trang, and Lam during their summer break from school. It wasn't a full-time job but depended on the company's work load for the week. There were many days I would bring the kids to work with me. I liked this. They could see how hard I worked, and they knew I expected them to work that hard too. My boss was pleased with this arrangement, and the kids were happy because they made some spending money. The only part they didn't like was getting out of bed so early in the morning. I didn't feel sorry for them. Getting up early and going to work was good for them.

In middle school Trang mostly had Asian friends, primarily those who spoke Vietnamese. By the time she was in high school, she had learned the language and was excelling in both sports and academics. She was confident in speaking English, and, although she still had her Vietnamese friends, she expanded her circle of friends to include some American kids. She won the state badminton title and was the captain of the tennis team. She took all sorts of advanced placement classes and tutored other students struggling with science. She had made friends with the academic-minded advanced placement students, the athletes and the science students she tutored. She earned a scholarship to continue her education at Augsburg College in St. Paul.

During Trang's first year of college, Grandpa Tran was diagnosed with cancer. Trang dropped out of school to take care of him as he traveled south to Texas to be with his brother. Six months later, she returned to Vietnam with him. He wanted to die in the country he had tried to defend from the communists, the country he loved so strongly.

Before Grandpa passed away, he insisted Trang return to the U.S.A. and get back to school. When she returned, her scholarship was gone. She picked up her college studies at Normandale Community College. When she had finished her Associate's degree, she began to work at Wells Fargo Bank and enrolled at Metro State University. She worked full time and took a full load of college courses. She graduated two years later with a degree in Finance. This made all of us very proud, our third college graduate.

66

OUR RELATIVES

The Vietnam War fractured our family. Those who survived ended up spread across the world. Each member of our family has a different, yet similar, story of immigration struggles and successes. If your family is all together in one location, take time to appreciate how lucky you are. It may not always be the case.

I left Vietnam and all of my family in 1979. Some of my family's stories have already been told but there are too many to tell in detail. These highlights will tell a little more of the story.

My second sister Liet lives in Australia. In 1982 her husband and two oldest girls escaped Vietnam and were sponsored by an organization in Australia. After a nine-year struggle, Liet and the three youngest were finally able to join them. By then her husband had

Me and Liet.

taken a new partner. Liet and the girls were forced to rent an apartment. The oldest girls left their father to live with their mother. Liet could not speak English but was able to take in sewing jobs at her home. Her oldest daughter, who was seventeen, went to high school and worked to help support her mother and sisters. In 1994 I went to

Australia to see my sister. I was thirty-four years old and had not seen Liet since I was a teenager.

My oldest sister, Danh, my second mother, is now in Minnesota. In 1985 her husband and oldest child escaped, and Becky and I were able to help them get a start in Minnesota. Twelve years later, Danh and her five younger children were finally able to join them. Now we are all together in Minnesota.

My brother Long and baby sister, Hoa, and their families have chosen to stay in Vietnam.

Becky, her parents and nine brothers and sisters all eventually escaped Vietnam. Everyone was safely relocated to various locations in the United States.

Becky's husband eventually escaped from Vietnam, settled in the U.S. where they were divorced. Becky's Catholic religion didn't allow for her to be remarried in the church. Being able to attend mass is very important to her, so we never married.

Son, Lam, and Trang have completed their bachelor's degrees. Tan is working on his.

In 2004 Son married Jennifer, an American woman. They chose to stay in Minnesota.

In 2005 Trang became an American citizen and sponsored her mother's (Hong's) immigration to Minnesota. They had not seen each other in fifteen years. For the first time in her life, Trang, her mother, and her father are living in the same country.

Trang.

The 270 of us that survived our boat trip from Vietnam were slowly relocated across the world. For the first five to ten years after we separated, we stayed in fairly close contact. As the years passed, we have drifted apart and into our own worlds.

The transition between the cultures is different for everyone that comes here. I was lucky, for I could embrace America and dive into this new world. When Trang and Grandpa arrived, we fixed Grandpa Tran up with his own apartment. Eventually his wife joined him. Grandpa Tran was an amazing person. After he lived here, he immediately sought out independent living, education, and employment. Grandma, on the other hand, never really blended into American culture. She was withdrawn and intimidated. Her work ethic was strong and so was her desire to help her family. Despite her fear of the new country and culture she found a job at Ragstock as a clothes sorter, a job that didn't require any English skills. She didn't try to learn English or integrate into the new culture. She kept to herself.

Trang misses her step-sister and has filled out the paperwork to get her to the United States. They say it is a ten-year wait.

My niece's wedding, 2002. Left to right: Tan, Lam, Becky, Thuy, Kiet, me, Jenny, and Son.

My family in Vietnam is shrinking little by little. As each of us are relocated across the world, the culture and traditions of my family are mixing with the cultures and traditions of those friends we make in our new countries. History tells us that this is what happened to Vietnam and to all countries throughout time. As people immigrate for whatever reason, they bring with them traits that influence their new countries. How interesting to experience the truth of history in my own lifetime. Most notable to me as a child was the Chinese and French influence on Vietnamese culture and traditions. Most notable to me now is my immediate family and the American influence on all of us.

Over the years I have observed that all discussion between refugees is in Vietnamese, our native language. Discussion between parents (refugees) and their children are in Vietnamese especially if it occurs in the house. Conversation amongst our children is most likely in English. We have to work hard to keep our language alive in America. It is very clear that my children have only rough Vietnamese language skills. Their Vietnamese skills remind me of my English skills, usable but not fluent. They can speak and listen in Vietnamese but barely read or write it. For me it is natural to speak Vietnamese. For my children, they prefer to speak English. For my grandchildren, we will see, but I expect their Vietnamese language to be limited to select phrases or sayings and much less integrated into their life.

Despite the long struggle to reunite my family, we feel lucky. Most of us survived the war, the escape, the refugee camps, and relocation. I cannot stand to think about the wars going on today in other countries and the legacy of sadness that is associated with them for years to come.

67

Everyday Life

Becky and I have blended into American life. Over the course of our twenties, thirties and forties, we raised our kids and made two more trips back to Vietnam. We've had several jobs and a few career changes, nothing drastically different than other Americans.

After working ten years assembling hearing aids for Maico, I needed a new challenge, and I left the company to work for Versa Electronics, a company that built circuit boards. The change was nice. After one year, I was offered a better opportunity, a chance to move off the assembly line with WaveCrest Technology.

WaveCrest did many of the same things as Versa. Instead of strictly assembly work, I worked directly with the design engineer. I frequently did the testing and the final build of the prototype board before it went back to the customer. Sometimes I did the build at WaveCrest, sometimes at our customer's facility. That was exciting. I was treated well, they paid for my travel expenses, and it made me feel important. WaveCrest had a corporate atmosphere that felt more like a family than a factory.

In 2002 as the electronic assembly industry crashed in Minnesota, I and many others lost our jobs at WaveCrest. Becky and I realized that electronics were moving out of Minnesota, and it was time for a career change. I decided to try my luck at owning and operating an Asian restaurant. Before I bought a restaurant, I worked as a cook to learn the business. When I felt I had enough experience, I bought a low-priced restaurant in Minneapolis. After three months of working night and day, I had no customers and no income. I sold the restaurant to someone else and ending up losing my investment money in the deal.

While I was experimenting with the restaurant business, Becky was laid off from her longtime job at Innovex. Things were not looking good for us. Becky started to look for a job in the electronics industry. I went fishing and tried to sort out my thoughts. One day after fishing at Bebe Lake in Hanover, I drove by a small building for sale on Highway 55 in Hamel, with no Asian restaurants anywhere near it and good visibility from the highway. After many lively discussions, Becky and I decided to rent the building and open up another restaurant. I started working all day and night with one hired person. We needed health insurance, and Becky was having trouble finding work, so I started looking. I found an electronics job at G.N. Resound, so we switched. Becky and a cook worked during the day, and Becky and I worked in the evening six days a week.

We named our restaurant the Rose Garden. We became good friends with our customers and built a good business. Our problem was we both had to be there every day. I needed some unrestricted time to go to Vietnam and see what I could learn of my father, I needed to move the graves of my mother and sister to a safe location; their "unofficial" cemetery was slated to be developed. Becky wanted to go to Texas to take care of her sick father. The only solution was to sell the restaurant. After five successful years in business, we sold the Rose Garden and went off to deal with family matters in different directions.

68

SEARCHING FOR CA

On my third trip back to Vietnam, I heard the radio and the newspaper stories about the psychic, Mr. Lien, who had reportedly been successful in linking people to their relatives lost in the war. Hanoi was a long trip, and to get in with the psychic would be difficult. Long and I called on Trinh, our solider friend from North Vietnam. The last time I saw Trinh was many years ago when he was in the hospital. Long said he had become a well-known person in the Vietnamese government. He was now the chairman of Labor and was based in Hanoi, the same city as Mr. Lien. Trinh was pleased to hear of my return and happy to be able to do us a favor. We didn't know how he did it, but Trinh arranged for a meeting with Mr. Lien.

Me and Trinh.

I was unable to go because my vacation was over. I needed to return to my electronics job in Minnesota. Long went to Hanoi and met with Mr. Lien.

The psychic told Long that there were two people who helped bury my father. He said my father was buried by the river next to a big tree. One of the people who buried my father was no longer alive, and the other was old but still living. This would be the person we must find in order to find my dad. Long started a search to find this person, but with the responsibilities of his family, his job, and injured son, he needed help. I put in my notice of resignation at my technician job and boarded a plane to Vietnam. This time I would not need to hurry home. This time I could stay as long as I was needed.

When I arrived in Vietnam, Long and I flew to Hanoi to meet with Trinh. Trinh arranged for a second meeting with Mr. Lien. We were thankful for this opportunity, but it didn't provide us much additional information. Before we left Hanoi, Trinh took out his private motor boat and brought us on a tour of the beautiful Ha Long Bay. It was a spectacular view of rock formations and caves set off by the bright blue sea water, an area of international tourist interest. The next day, Long and I returned to Nha Trang to try to find our missing father, Ca Nguyen.

Our first task was to find the person who buried our father. It was difficult, seemingly impossible. We started asking everyone we could who might have been near the North Vietnam base and prison camp. Out of the blue, Tu contacted us. Her nephew worked for Long and heard about the search for our father's body. Tu was a messenger who carried information and goods between the camps and villages during the war. Although she didn't know my father directly she knew of the location of the camp and of other people who worked at the camp. With the help of Tu, we met Dong. Dong was a nurse in the NVA prison camp located on the mountain. Dong told us that it took ten days of walking for prisoners from my village to reach the camp. He said the prisoners were only allowed to move during the night, through the jungle without the aid of light. This was to keep them hidden from airplanes flying over the jungle. Dong remembered my dad. My dad was fairly well known as he was the mayor of our village. He said he was not shot as I was told by cousin Ra, but that my dad became sick and died at the camp. Dong remembered where he was buried.

We were overwhelmed with emotion after talking to Dong about our dad. My body was shaking. Long had tears running down his cheek. The search for our dad might have an ending. Dong told us to assemble a search party of fourteen. The place where we would find my father was in a remote area on the mountain. An area filled with vegetation and an area where no one lived. We would need food and shelter for living in the jungle. We would need shovels and a hired guard to protect us from harm. We would need a guide. Dong was the only person who would know exactly where to dig. To our dismay Dong told us he was not able to hike to the mountain. He had a leg injury from the war that made it difficult for him to walk. He was also too old to hike through the jungle. We couldn't believe this bad news. We stared at him in disbelief. We had just found the person who could bring us to our father, but he couldn't join the search party. Dong offered to draw us a map, and he did so in the best detail he could remember. Without any words spoken, Dong, Long, and I knew it would be difficult to find this spot. The jungle grows and changes quickly. To find a location from thirty-four years earlier would be like finding a grain of rice in the ocean. Yet, this was our best chance, and we knew we had to try to find our father.

The news of my father being sick and dying in camp surprised us. For the past thirty years, we believed that he had been shot trying to escape. This turn of events still occupies my thoughts today as I try to recreate, in my own mind, the end of my father's life and understand what happened to him.

Long and I wasted no time. We hired a search party that would be led by Tu, the woman who was a messenger and traveled this route frequently, albeit many years ago. We hired an armed guard and several men to carry supplies. We met in Nha Trang and drove to Thanh City. Thanh City was not really a city at all but a small settlement of indigenous Vietnamese people up in the mountain. This is where the road ended, and this is where our difficult hike would begin.

Our hike was something that would best be covered by *National Geographic*. We first had to cross a stream swollen with water from the rainy season. The current was too strong to walk across it unaided, so we cut bamboo to construct a railing. With difficulty, we laid it across the river and held onto it to keep our balance as we moved through the rapid current. We were all wet and so were most of our supplies by the time we reached the other side. From the river, we followed Tu through the jungle. I wore my western hiking boots but the rest of the party wore open sandals, the type of shoe worn everyday in Vietnam. They had no socks, no support, and no protection or traction. The younger men in our party cut the thick jungle vegetation as we walked, not for every step, but often to allow us passage. The path that existed thirty years ago no longer was visible. We wound our way up the mountain slowly. There was no vista, only plants in front of our eyes and humid thick air to breathe.

Our hike continued for six hours. I was the last one and often the group would have to wait for me. I was thin and in fairly good shape but I was not used to hiking in the mountains. Eventually we reached the location we believed Dong had marked on the map and set up camp nearby. Hammocks were hung from the trees in a long row and an area was cleared for a fire. We spent the rest of this day getting organized for the upcoming days of digging. We made a fire, ate, drank and discussed our plans. Camping in the jungle was spooky at best. I made sure my hammock was in the middle of the group so the wild animals would not find me first. Standing or sitting in this area was painful. The ants were everywhere—red, yellow and black ants in every size and shape. They would crawl up our legs so fast and bite. I brought bug spray with me from Minnesota. No one else had ever seen this before. I think it helped some with the flying and biting in-sects, but they were everywhere. As I lay on my hammock that first night, the dark consumed me. I had not been exposed to such absolute darkness since those terrifying days on the wooden escape boat. Some-where in the depths of my soul I started humming, that familiar tune. My mother was with me that night.

We woke at morning light, ate some rice and tried to figure out where to start digging. The young men cleared an area so we could see the ground. Before the ground was broken, we lit incense and prayed. Long and I both prayed out loud to our God for help in finding our father. Then the digging started. The shovels we brought were quite different from western shovels. They resembled large hoes. We carried the metal blades and then cut bamboo handles for them at the site. The digging continued for several days, but we found nothing. After our fifth night of camping, our food supply was running low and so was our hope. As far as we could tell, we were at the location mapped by Dong. Beyond that, Tu was not able to give us further advice. She had not been involved in burying my father nor was anyone else in the search party. Finally I had to make the decision, the very hard de-cision, of ending the search and returning to Thanh City. It was a tired and demoralized group that hiked down the mountain and across the river to Thanh City.

Everyone was frustrated with our search efforts, Long and I were exhausted and anxious to return home to rest. My legs ached so badly, I thought I would never walk again. We wrestled with our situation and what we should do. Neither of us wanted to give up on our dad when it seemed we were so close to finding him. Would I be able to hike up the mountain again? Could Dong give us a better map? We decided we must see Dong and talk to him, and that is what we did. At Dong's house we recounted our trip and tried to explain where we went. It was impossible for us to explain exactly where we went in the jungle. It was confusing and frustrating to all of us. I was impatient. I begged Dong to travel with us. He was our only hope, the only one that would be able to recognize where my father was buried. Dong wasn't physically able to handle the rigors of that sort of trip. We all could see that. Amazingly he agreed to come with us if we hired people to carry him. He thought he could walk a little but would need to be carried much of the way. We were relieved and overjoyed at the prospect of bringing Dong with us and were inspired by his courage.

FINDING CA

We set about rounding up our search party again. Tu surprised us by wanting to join us for the second mission. Tu was in her sixties and was by far the oldest person in our first group. This time Dong would be the oldest. We hired the entire crew again, knowing this time the young strong men would also have to help carry Dong. We bought more supplies and developed a new plan. It was only two days later that we set out for the mountain. During this period of time, I felt like I was on a rollercoaster. I felt tired, anxious, excited, scared and filled with anticipation.

Our second trip started much like the first with a drive to Thanh City. The mood of the group was a little subdued compared to our first adventure. Long and I were hopeful that we would be successful with Dong along, but the others seemed more quiet, perhaps they were tired from our last outing, probably discouraged with our outcome. In any case we were back at it. This time in Thanh City we rented a wagon, a jeep-like vehicle, and we were able to drive the crew one hour further into the jungle.

With Dong along, the hike was slow. The slower pace was good for me. I was able to keep up with the group this time. We followed the same path, so we had less cutting to do to get to our camp. We set up camp in the same location. Dong assured us this was correct. We had indeed followed his instructions properly last time. Once we unpacked, Long and I lit the incense and prayed for the return of our father. Our group spent the rest of this day setting up camp and cooking dinner.

By the light of the new day, Dong was able to locate the large tree that he had told us about. It wasn't all that far from where we were digging on the previous trip. The crew cleared away the vegetation from the base of the tree and the digging began. The crew had nearly excavated around the entire perimeter of this tree when one of the workers spotted something, a bone. Excitement rose as everyone gathered to look. We gently dug and collected up the remains of my father. We brought a special plastic bag along with us to carry my father's remains home. His remains had returned to the earth over the years, and the pieces we could still recover fit into a small brief case. The discovery sent a surge of power through all of us. A newly energized crew carefully worked on this important task.

Memories of my father's life and mine and the series of events that brought us to the mountain that day ran full speed through my mind. The crew said no one had ever done this before. No one had hired a search party to look for their missing family. Dong and Tu both told me my dad would be honored that I did not give up on him. To me it felt like I had no choice. I was born into the Vietnam War, and it influenced everything I had ever done.

We held a ceremony for my dad that night in the jungle. A special meal was offered to him as we do in traditional Vietnamese funeral ceremonies. We later held a feast for the search crew. This would be our only night of camping on the mountain. There was no need to conserve our supplies. We were all filled with a great sense of accomplishment and pride. As I lay in my hammock that night, the pitch black sky did not seem as scary and isolating. It covered me in a blanket of peace.

70

AT REST

We returned to Nha Trang where news of our adventure traveled fast. We were victorious; we had conquered the odds. We found Ca and returned him home. Long and I met with the leaders of the temple in Nha Trang. We arranged for my father to be cremated and for a proper funeral service to be held. Cremation was a newer idea in Vietnam but seemed appropriate for this situation. The funeral service was spread over three days. During this time, our family and friends from around the area gathered at the temple. On the first day, we brought my dad's ashes to the temple and put him in his new resting spot, his new home. A beautiful stone plaque was carved and placed on the outside wall of the temple. The ashes were placed in the space behind it for safe keeping. This day we also said many prayers in his honor. On the second day, we continued to

At the Nha Trang temple. Two young brothers, my father, Ca Nguyen, my mother, Ly Thi Kinh, and sister Nguyet.

182

pray for him and held a feast in his honor. On the third day, we prayed for him and cleaned the temple. We made sure everything was done properly so the memorial service could be completed. This is the temple where we would place my mother and sister when we needed to move them from the cemetery. This was the place where everyone would meet again.

My duties in Vietnam were over. It was time for me to go back to America.

71

The End

I flew back to Minnesota, tired and emotionally drained. I had conquered the monster. I had returned my dad to his family, and now I could return to my family. The book you are reading has been my way of healing from the inside out. It is a way for me to tell my children and grandchildren about my life. I have a need for them to understand more about my life and the series of events that have given them a life of privilege in America.

People call me a survivor, but I know I wouldn't have had a chance without the troops and allies of the South Army, the people across the world that helped others in need, my God, and my family.

My fiftieth birthday. "I am fifty years old, the year my story was published. Celebrating are friend Jeff, Becky, me, friend Carolyn, and Connie, the book writer.

FAMILY TREE

Ca Nguyen – Trong's father
Kinh Thi Ly – Trong's mother

Oanh – Trong's oldest sister
Liet – Trong's second sister
Long – Trong's older brother
Nguyet – Trong's third sister
Trong – fifth child
Hoa – Trong's younger sister

Becky – Trong's partner
Son – Becky's older son
Lam – Becky's younger son
Trang – Trong's daughter
Tan – Becky and Trong's son

Hong – Trong's former girlfriend, Trang's mother.
Grandpa Tran – Hong's father, Trang's grandfather
Loc, Thanh and Hanh – Trong's Cousins
Jeanne Teigen – Trong's American mom